ROUTLEDGE LIBRARY EDITIONS:
THE MEDIEVAL WORLD

Volume 48

EXPLORING CASTLES

EXPLORING CASTLES

W. DOUGLAS SIMPSON

LONDON AND NEW YORK

First published in 1957 by Routledge & Kegan Paul Limited

This edition first published in 2020
by Routledge
2 Park Square, Milton Park, Abingdon, Oxon OX14 4RN

and by Routledge
52 Vanderbilt Avenue, New York, NY 10017

Routledge is an imprint of the Taylor & Francis Group, an informa business

©1957 Routledge & Kegan Paul Limited

All rights reserved. No part of this book may be reprinted or reproduced or utilised in any form or by any electronic, mechanical, or other means, now known or hereafter invented, including photocopying and recording, or in any information storage or retrieval system, without permission in writing from the publishers.

Trademark notice: Product or corporate names may be trademarks or registered trademarks, and are used only for identification and explanation without intent to infringe.

British Library Cataloguing in Publication Data
A catalogue record for this book is available from the British Library

ISBN: 978-0-367-22090-7 (Set)
ISBN: 978-0-429-27322-3 (Set) (ebk)
ISBN: 978-0-367-19550-2 (Volume 48) (hbk)
ISBN: 978-0-367-19556-4 (Volume 48) (pbk)
ISBN: 978-0-429-20314-5 (Volume 48) (ebk)

Publisher's Note
The publisher has gone to great lengths to ensure the quality of this reprint but points out that some imperfections in the original copies may be apparent.

Disclaimer
The publisher has made every effort to trace copyright holders and would welcome correspondence from those they have been unable to trace.

EXPLORING CASTLES

by
W. DOUGLAS SIMPSON

Routledge & Kegan Paul
LONDON

First published 1957
© *by Routledge & Kegan Paul Limited*
Broadway House, Carter Lane, E.C.4
Printed in Great Britain
by Western Printing Services Ltd, Bristol

To the memory of
HERBERT LEWIS HONEYMAN
and
BRYAN HUGH ST. JOHN O'NEIL
with whom I have explored many castles

Contents

	ACKNOWLEDGEMENTS	xi
I	WHAT CASTLES WERE, AND HOW THEY CAME INTO BRITAIN	1
II	CASTLES OF EARTHWORK AND WOOD	4
III	GREAT STONE TOWERS AND SHELL-KEEPS	10
IV	HOW CASTLES WERE ATTACKED AND DEFENDED	20
V	EXPLORING A NORMAN CASTLE	28
VI	COURTYARD CASTLES AND FORTIFIED MANOR-HOUSES	42
VII	THE EDWARDIAN CASTLES	56
VIII	MORE ABOUT EDWARDIAN CASTLES	69
IX	THE TOWER OF LONDON: AND WINDSOR CASTLE	86
X	NORTHERN TOWER-HOUSES	98
XI	'BASTARD FEUDALISM' AND A NEW KIND OF CASTLE	115
XII	THE TWILIGHT OF CASTLES IN ENGLAND	133
XIII	THE INDIAN SUMMER OF THE SCOTTISH CASTLE	147
XIV	'GOTHICK' AND MODERN CASTLES	153
	INDEX	159

Illustrations

FIGURES

1 Pleshey Castle: plan	page 5
2 Hedingham: plan of ground floor	13
3 Rochester: interior view of keep	17
4 Siege of a Castle, showing the use of a 'belfry', a 'cat' and 'pavises', and catapults	21
5 Attack on a Castle with a 'belfry'	23
6 Newcastle-on-Tyne: plan of Norman earthwork castle	29
7 Newcastle-upon-Tyne: plan of keep at second-floor level	32
8 Newcastle-upon-Tyne: plan of keep at first-floor level	34
9 Newcastle-upon-Tyne: plan of keep at ground-floor level	37
10 Newcastle-upon-Tyne: plan of keep at roof level	38
11 Newcastle-upon-Tyne: section through keep looking south	40
12 The Château de Loches, a French castle showing Norman keep enclosed with a curtain wall and round towers in the thirteenth century	44
13 Pevensey Castle: curtain walls and towers of the thirteenth century	46
14 Conisborough: general view, showing keep, curtain wall and round towers	47
15 Bothwell Castle: a Scottish round keep	48
16 Flint Castle: general plan	58
17 Harlech Castle: general plan	60
18 Beaumaris Castle: general plan	63

ILLUSTRATIONS

19 Caernarvon Castle: general plan *page* 64
20 Caerphilly Castle: general plan 67
21 Tonbridge Castle: general plan 72
22 Tonbridge Castle: plans of gatehouse 74
23 Llanstephan: sketch plan 79
24 Dunstanburgh Castle: sketch plan 81
25 Belsay Castle: first-floor plan 108
26 Borthwick Castle: plan of first floor 110
27 Coxton Tower: plans and sections 112
28 Doune Castle: plans 123
29 Muness Castle: plans 158

PLATES

facing page

1 Pevensey Castle. The Roman wall and towers 32
2 The keep of the Castle of Newcastle-upon-Tyne 33
3 Framlingham Castle, from north-west 48
4 Harlech Castle: general view from the south, with Snowdon behind 49
5 Caernarvon Castle, from the south 64
6 Windsor Castle: aerial view from the west 65
7 Greenknowe Tower: view from south-east 80
8 Coxton Tower: view from south-west 81
9 Bodiam Castle: aerial view from the south 96
10 Doune Castle: general view from the north-east 97
11 Tattershall Castle: view of great tower from south-west 112
12 Corfe Castle: general view from the south-east 113
13 Muness Castle: view from south-east 128
14 Noltland Castle: view from south-east 129
15 Craigievar Castle: view from north-west 144
16 Iron Yett at Barns Castle, Peebleshire 145

Acknowledgements

Plates 1, 3 and 5, and Figures 1, 18, 19 and 24 are reproduced by courtesy of the Ministry of Works and H.M. Stationery Office.

Plate 2 from a photograph supplied by Messrs. Philipson and Son Ltd., Newcastle-uopn-Tyne.

Plate 4 from a photograph by Mr. J. Dixon Scott, by courtesy of *Archaeologia Cambrensis*.

Plates 6 and 9 by courtesy of *Country Life*.

Plate 12, and Figures 16 and 20 by courtesy of Mr. Sidney Toy, F.S.A., and Messrs. Heinemann.

Plates 13 and 14, and Figure 29 by courtesy of the Third Spalding Club.

Plates 7, 8, 10, 11, 15 and 16 by courtesy of Aberdeen University Library.

Figures 2, 3, 12, 13, 14, 15, 17, 21, 22, 23, 27 and 28 are reproduced from drawings in Aberdeen University Library.

Figures 3, 12, 13 and 14 were drawn by the late David MacGibbon, LL.D., and Figure 15 by the late Thomas Ross, LL.D., H.R.S.A.

Figures 4 and 5 are reproduced from Viollet-le-Duc, *Dictionnaire Raisonné de l'Architecture Française*.

The blocks for Figures 6-11 and 25 were kindly lent by the Society of Antiquaries of Newcastle-upon-Tyne.

Figure 26 is reproduced by courtesy of the Royal Commission on Historical Monuments (Scotland).

I
What Castles Were, and How they Came into Britain

Most people enjoy looking at ancient castles. Sometimes they are gaunt and desolate storm-beaten ruins upon which the wind and the rain have exerted their fury unresisted for generations; or they may still stand erect and proud, and it may be that those who live in them are the lineal descendants of its ancient lords. Sometimes there is nothing but a great green mound, with a deep ditch round it; and this is not because the stone buildings have disappeared, but because there never were any—for the earliest castles were all made, not of stone and lime but of earth and wood.

I chiefly enjoy ruined castles, rather than those which are still inhabited or the ones which are nothing but earthen mounds. To begin with, our ruined castles are such lovely things to look at.

> Time . . .
> has mouldered into beauty many a tower
> Which, when it frowned with all its battlements
> Was only terrible.[1]

And one can try to understand the meaning of these old ruins: to picture them as places in which people once dwelt, to clothe their desolate halls with tapestry and fill their emptiness with all the life of those days; to puzzle out their plan when blurred by decay, to give its proper meaning to each vault, passage or winding stairway. When we look at castles in this way, we recall that they were the dwelling places of our forebears, men and women with their problems. There is pleasure in tracing how they strove

[1] William Mason, *The English Garden*, Book I.

to reconcile the two clashing needs of defence and comfort: how, as the country became more peaceful, the military aspect of the castle yielded place to the domestic, and the grim fortalice grew into a fair mansion.

There is also the historic interest of these time-worn buildings. Each has its story or its ballad—sad and terrible memories, some of them, of the olden days of sturt and broil. The grim vaults and gloomy dungeons which form their lower parts have sometimes witnessed fearful scenes, and the terror of forgotten anguish still hushes our laughter as we descend into them. But all their history is not made up of horror and iniquity; and many ancient castles have been the scene of brightness and triumph.

Castles were introduced into this country by the Normans. Everyone knows how that race of mounted, mail-clad warriors came over under their leader, William the Conqueror, and struck down the English at the Battle of Hastings in 1066; how William had himself crowned King of England, and very soon overran the whole country. These Normans brought with them the system of government called feudalism; and to understand what a castle was, one must understand this system of feudalism.

A thousand years ago there were no trained civil servants scattered over the country. There were no rapid means of communication, no wireless, telephone, telegraph, or railways. The roads were few and bad, and travelling was so slow that it took a week to go from London to Newcastle. Moreover, the country was full of lawless characters, and wayfarers were in constant peril of being robbed or even killed upon the highroads.

Under these conditions it was difficult for the King in London to have his orders obeyed, and the work of government carried on, in outlying districts. So he had to enlist the help of the great lords who were on the spot—powerful men strong enough to bring the King's government to a standstill unless he made some sort of a bargain with them. But to make a bargain you must have something to bargain with. In those days the principal wealth was land, and the King claimed to be supreme owner of all the land in the kingdom. So he made a kind of bargain with the great landowners. 'I will allow you to hold your estates,' it said in effect, 'provided you become my "vassal"': you must acknowledge me as your overlord and hold your lands as my tenant. In return

WHAT CASTLES WERE

I will support you against your enemies. But you on your part must accept the responsibility for governing your tenants on my behalf. You must administer justice among them in your "barony courts", and in time of war you must assemble the able-bodied men among your tenants under your own banner and lead them to join my army.

So feudalism was a system whereby ownership of land went hand in hand with responsibility for military defence and local government. Nowadays on a country estate a landlord's relations with his tenants are largely economic. The tenants have to pay rent, and the landlord in return has to keep their farm steadings in order and has other duties towards them. But he is no longer their military leader in time of war, nor does he do justice among them in his private courts. The State now manages these things itself, and deals in such matters direct with its individual subjects. It calls them up if they are liable for military service, and it deals justice among them in the public law courts.

Feudalism of course gave the landlords great power over their tenants; and under a weak king, the feudal system often resulted in bitter oppression of the small man by the great man. Of this new system the castle, as the private stronghold of a feudal baron, was the visible symbol. It was not a purely State concern like the forts built in Britain by the old Roman Empire, or those that now defend our ports and shores. Nor yet was it simply a landowner's residence, like the squire's hall or laird's house that we know. In fact it was a little of both—the fortified residence of a landowner and a centre of local government. Fortified it had to be, in those times when baron fought with baron and private wars were common. And in his 'barony courts', often held in the great hall of the castle, the feudal lord dealt justice out to his tenants, both in civil and in criminal cases—in disputes about property or offences against the law. In the latter, the great lords, at least in earlier times, had full powers of delegated royal justice over their vassals. They could imprison them in the castle 'pit' or dungeon, they could put them to death upon the castle gibbet. This is what is understood by 'the right of pit and gallows'. But in all such cases the feudal landlord was supposed to be acting as representative of the King.

So castles appeared in this country, along with the feudal system, through the Norman conquerors. The next point to discuss is the nature of these early Norman castles.

II
Castles of Earthwork and Wood

ONE is apt to think of a Norman castle as a ponderous square tower of stone, like the Tower of London, or the great Norman keeps at Rochester, or Newcastle-upon-Tyne, or Castle Hedingham in Essex, or Norham on the Tweed. Probably it was Sir Walter Scott who started this idea of the Norman baron dwelling in such vast and gloomy towers. Scott wrote in *Ivanhoe* an exciting account of the siege of Torquilstone Castle, the stronghold of the cruel and tyrannical Norman baron, Sir Reginald Front-de-Boeuf. Torquilstone is pictured as one of these great square stone towers, with outer walls and palisades.

But these square stone keeps were by no means the typical strongholds of the Norman conquerors. In those early days such a large stone structure cost a great deal of money. Only the kings themselves, who built the Tower of London and the keep at Newcastle, or the greatest and wealthiest among their barons, like the de Veres of Hedingham, could afford to build such costly residences. The ordinary Norman baron, who had not money enough to build himself a great stone tower, used different materials for his castle. Instead of making it of stone and lime, he made it of earthwork and timber.

What happened was this. He dug a great circular ditch, and the earth which he thus took out he heaped up in the centre so as to form a tall, conical, flat-topped mound. Round the edge of its summit he set a palisade of stout tree-trunks; and within the palisade he built a tall wooden tower. The whole of this structure, the moated mound with its palisade on top and wooden tower within the palisade, formed the lord's residence in time of peace, and in time of war became the citadel of the castle.

Attached to this moated mound, in the larger castles at least, there was usually a courtyard enclosure, defended by a palisaded

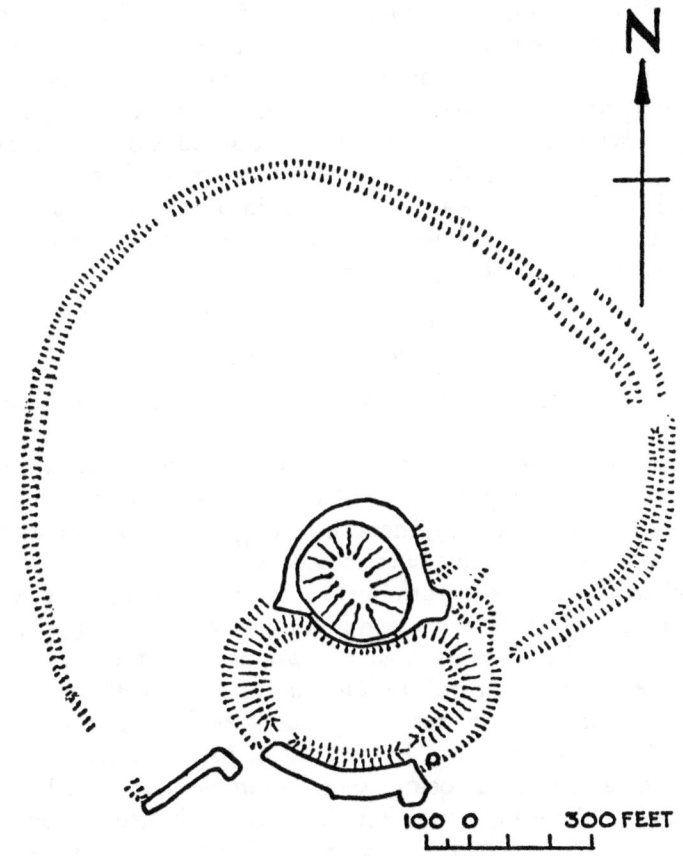

FIG. 1. Pleshey Castle: plan.

bank and ditch. This sheltered the domestic buildings of the lord's household—the hall, chapel, stables, barn, byre, and so forth. All these buildings were of wood, or of wattle and daub, or similar materials. They were dominated by the lord's wooden tower on the mound, which could still be defended even if the courtyard had been captured.

CASTLES OF EARTHWORK AND WOOD

The Norman name for such a mound was *motte*, and the courtyard enclosure was styled the bailey (Fig. 1). So the complete examples of this kind of structure are known as *motte* and bailey castles.

Of course, such castles varied greatly in size, according to the owner's requirements or purse. Some of the smaller ones never had a bailey. And equally if a natural mound was handy the Norman baron would use it, cutting it to the size and shape he wanted.

Living as I do in a seaside town, when I was a child we used to go down to the beach to play. Here, at the edge of the incoming water, we used to heap up a great mound of sand, with a ditch round it. When the sea-water flowed into and filled our moat, one of us would stand on top of the mound and try to keep the others off with his spade, chanting:

'I'm the King of the Castle
And you're the dirty rascal!'

I did not then know that we were really making a Norman castle.

One should not imagine that these wooden castles were intended to be temporary, or that they were poor affairs for defence. On the contrary, they were designed as permanent fortifications, and formidable ones. It was exceedingly difficult for the attackers, clad in heavy armour, to cross the ditch, to scale the smooth slopes of the *motte*, and pull to pieces the strong palisade on its summit. It is true that the wooden buildings inside the palisade could be set on fire. On the other hand, they could be quickly and cheaply replaced. The wooden superstructures have long since perished, but the earthworks endure, and some of them are very imposing. Good examples are found at the castles of Tonbridge in Kent, Tickhill in Northamptonshire, Lewes and Arundel in Sussex, Shrewsbury in Shropshire, and in many other places. Wales has some fine specimens, such as the great *motte* at Cardiff. In parts of Scotland where the Normans settled we meet with these characteristic earthworks, like the Mote of Urr, in Galloway, the Doune of Invernochty in Aberdeenshire, or the Castle of Duffus in Moray.

Antiquaries, digging on the summits of these mounds, are sometimes lucky enough to discover the postholes of the pali-

CASTLES OF EARTHWORK AND WOOD

sades and of the wooden tower inside. And there are illustrations of these earth and timber castles in the Bayeux Tapestry, which tells the story of the Norman Conquest in a series of seventy-two delightful needlework pictures. In one of these pictures, the Conqueror's pioneers are shaping the mound of Hastings Castle, and the Latin inscription which explains the scene runs thus, in translation: William 'ordered that a castle should be'—not *built* but '*dug* at Hastings'.

Travelling about the country in search of these Norman earthworks, one will find that time and again the Norman *motte* is close by a parish church. And for this there is a very good reason. When a Norman baron settled down on his new estate, first of all he built a castle for himself. Then, close beside it, he built a chapel for the spiritual needs of his household and dependants. Very often, the priest who served in the chapel would be a younger brother or younger son of the Norman lord. In due course, it frequently happened that the lord's estate or manor became a parish, and sometimes the curious boundaries of parishes today can be shown to have been due to the fact that they were originally the 'marches' of a Norman manor. In such cases the private chapel of the lord would become the parish church. Manor and parish, castle and church, have in such cases usually had a common origin.

Quaint and imperfect as they are, the representations of these tall wooden castles on their moated mounds, which we can still look at in the Bayeux Tapestry, show that they must have been picturesque structures, utterly unlike anything that we can readily conceive of today. Moreover their timber-work was brightly coloured.

Sometimes in later days great stone towers and walls were erected on top of these Norman earthworks. Rearing such ponderous structures on artificial mounds could have disastrous results. This can be seen at Duffus Castle in Morayshire, where in the fourteenth century a great stone tower was built upon the *motte*, and thick "curtain" or enclosing walls drawn round the bailey. Large sections of these walls have slipped down the bank, and on the *motte* a whole corner of the tower has broken off and skidded body-bulk down the slope, coming to rest at a fantastic angle, with all its windows and wall-chambers in perfect preservation—a notable tribute to the stout old masonry.

CASTLES OF EARTHWORK AND WOOD

In other cases where the early wooden superstructures have been replaced in stone, the result has been some of the noblest among British castles. Anyone making the railway journey between England and Scotland by day, using the east coast route, will have seen the towering mass of Durham Castle, with the vast bulk of the Norman cathedral close beside it—both enclosed in a great loop of the River Wear, flowing in a deep valley round the site. This great castle of Durham, which now houses the university, is nothing more than a *motte* and bailey castle, refashioned in stone. Here, on a grander scale perhaps than anywhere else in the world, we have the characteristic Norman presence of church and castle side by side. At Durham also there has been much trouble with the foundations, and a great deal of money has had to be spent in underpinning them.

In some ways the noblest castle in Britain is Windsor. Here from the outset there are two baileys, with a great *motte* between them. On the top of the *motte*, Edward III reared a great circular tower, which still stands, though much rebuilt. The two baileys were also, in course of time, encircled with walls and towers, and within them are many stately buildings including St. George's Chapel, where kings and queens are buried. As far back as the thirteenth century, Windsor Castle could be described as 'the most splendid building within the bounds of Europe'.

In Norman times, no one was supposed to build a castle without a licence from the King. During the miserable reign of King Stephen (1135–54), when the country fell into confusion and the Norman barons did as they liked, it is said that no less than 1,117 of these unlicensed castles were built in England. The great majority were of the earth and timber type, and the remains of not a few of them may still be seen up and down the country. In these castles the Norman barons, unrestrained by the King, wrought many cruel deeds. An old English chronicler, in a famous passage, has described some of the horrors of that awful time:

'Every powerful man made his castles: and they filled the land full of castles. They cruelly oppressed the wretched men of the land with castle-works.[1] When the castles were made they filled

---

[1] This means that the Saxon peasantry had to heap up the castle mounds and construct their timber buildings by forced labour for their Norman masters.

CASTLES OF EARTHWORK AND WOOD

them with devils and evil men. Then took they those men that they imagined had any property, both by night and by day, peasant men and women, and put them in prison for their gold and silver, and tortured them with unutterable torture: for never were martyrs so tortured as they were.'[1]

Often beside the Norman earthworks one finds a place name or place names which tell that there was once a castle here. Thus the word *Castleton*, so often found at the site of a *motte* and bailey, means the *tun* or farm of the castle, which the lord held in his own hands and cultivated for his own household. It is the home farm, as one would say now. In Scotland the corresponding word is *Mains*, from the Latin phrase *terra mensalis*, the *mensal* land, the land from whose produce the lord supplied his *mensa* or table. Sometimes also in Scotland the word is *Bordland*, for boardland, again referring to the lord's table—in much the same way as we still speak of 'board and lodging'. Words like Castleton, Mains and Bordland— or Borland, as it has sometimes become—furnish proof of the former presence of a castle, even although both earthwork and stone may have long since vanished. *Ingliston*, the town or farm of the English, is likewise a name frequently found in Scotland beside the earthworks of an early castle. It recalls the Anglo-Norman immigrants who built their stronghold in a Celtic land. Many of the castle-builders in Scotland were Flemings, pioneers of the wool industry. So *Flemington* or *Flanders* or *Flinders* are names sometimes found near an ancient moated mount.

[1] From the *Anglo-Saxon Chronicle*, under the year 1137.

III

Great Stone Towers and Shell-keeps

In the year 410 the Roman government withdrew its soldiers from Britain, leaving the island a prey to Angles and Saxons, who in two centuries of bitter warfare overcame the romanized Britons and changed the name of their country into England.

The Romans lumped together all those peoples who invaded them under the general name of barbarians. But that meant no more than that they did not speak Greek or Latin, the two civilized languages of the Roman Empire. It did not at all mean that they were savages. Alaric the Goth was a Christian and a gentleman, and even the Angles and the Saxons, who were certainly the fiercest of the various tribes who overthrew the Roman Empire, were not barbarians in any modern use of the word. Much evidence of an advanced way of life was found in the grave of an unknown East Anglian prince, which was discovered in 1939 at Sutton Hoo, near Woodbridge in Suffolk. The man buried there with such splendid furnishings was certainly no savage.

The houses where these early Teutonic settlers lived were quite different from the mansions of their Roman predecessors. A Roman gentleman's country house was usually arranged round two or more sides of a courtyard, and contained a number of rooms each assigned to a distinct purpose, as in most of our houses today. In strong contrast, the early Teutonic war-lord built himself a single huge timber hall, which served all the purposes of his household. Here they cooked, ate and drank, worked, played, and slept more or less all together. Such a hall with its imposing span of roof expressed the chief's pride among the huts of his dependants

GREAT STONE TOWERS AND SHELL-KEEPS

clustered around. There is nothing more grand than a great hall, such as one may still see at Christ Church, Oxford, or at Westminster.

Life in a single room, however large, could have had little privacy and certainly had much inconvenience. As civilization grew, attempts were made to improve the accommodation. At one end of the hall a separate kitchen, pantry and so forth were added. At the other end, private apartments were set aside for the lord and his family and their distinguished guests. This end of the hall was usually provided with a low raised platform, called the 'dais', upon which the high table was set at right angles to the body of the hall. At the high table sat the lord and his family with their personal guests, while the rank and file of the household ate from the trestle boards stretching lengthwise down the hall. Towards the end of the feast, the party at the high table withdrew into the 'solar' or withdrawing room behind, leaving the rest of the company to finish their meal and then to clear up. The lower end of the hall was shut off by a timber screen, so as to deaden the noise of cooking in the kitchen and to provide a place for loading the various dishes. Above the 'screens', as this lower end of the hall came to be called, was a music gallery, where the minstrels played, directly opposite the company at the high table at the upper end of the hall. These arrangements still exist in most of the Oxford and Cambridge college halls to this day.

Such a house, based on the idea of a central hall, was known as a hall-house. It is because the early squires' houses in England were built upon this plan that the manor-house of an English estate is commonly known as the Hall, whatever its plan and architectural style now may be. One may find in *Ivanhoe*, in Cedric the Saxon's manor-house of Rotherwood, a brilliant picture of a timber-built old English hall-house.

In the Latin of those days, such a hall-house was called a *palatium*. In its origin the word 'palace' simply denotes a hall-house, irrespective of its size or who lives in it. Down to quite a late date it was regularly so used in Scotland, where the term 'palace', or 'house built palace-wise', means nothing more than a hall-house—in Scottish speech, a 'ha' hoose'—and is used of any such structure, whether large or small.

At first the early Teutonic conquerors of the Roman Empire

GREAT STONE TOWERS AND SHELL-KEEPS

built their halls of timber. Very soon, however, they learned from their Roman subjects the art of building in stone and lime, and began to construct their palaces, or hall-houses, of solid masonry. It is certain that the Anglo-Saxons possessed a few such stone halls, though none of them now exist. But we still have some very fine Norman stone halls. Noblest of all is Westminster Hall—though it was cased with new stonework, inside and outside, and otherwise remodelled, in the reign of Richard II. It measures about 230 feet long and 130 broad.

In the ninth century, when the Frankish Empire began to decay, and all northern Europe was exposed to the ravages of the Vikings, these great timber halls were found to be vulnerable to attack. It became necessary to devise a more defensible sort of dwelling. This problem was solved in a very simple and ingenious manner. The wooden house was up-ended. Its rooms were arranged in the same order, but instead of being extended horizontally along the ground, they were piled one on top of another. The common hall remained the central structure, but the kitchen, pantry and cellars were placed *below* it instead of at one end, and the lord's private room and sleeping apartment *above* the hall instead of at its upper end. Thus the *hall-house* was transformed into a *tower-house*. Its lofty narrow structure offered a much smaller frontage of timber for the assailants to seek to cut through or to set on fire. The defenders on top of the tower were less exposed to the arrows of those below, and better able to destroy them by hurling down missiles on their heads. And the lord's own rooms could now be reached only by climbing narrow stairs or ladders.

Once experience had pointed out these advantages, everywhere in northern France the lords began to build themselves towerhouses instead of hall-houses. The growth of feudalism led to incessant private warfare between neighbouring landowners, and this in its turn drove them to seek still more security for their dwellings. So they began to erect their wooden tower-houses on the top of conical mounds, thus making it less easy for their enemies to get at them. This is how the Norman *motte* castle, with its timber tower, originated.

While the great majority of tower-houses continued to be made of wood, or sometimes of wattle and daub, or of hard,

GREAT STONE TOWERS AND SHELL-KEEPS

compacted clay strengthened by fascines or hurdle work, there were also tower-houses built of stone and lime. Mostly, owing to their weight, these were erected on the natural ground, not on the mottes or artificial mounds which were not strong enough to bear

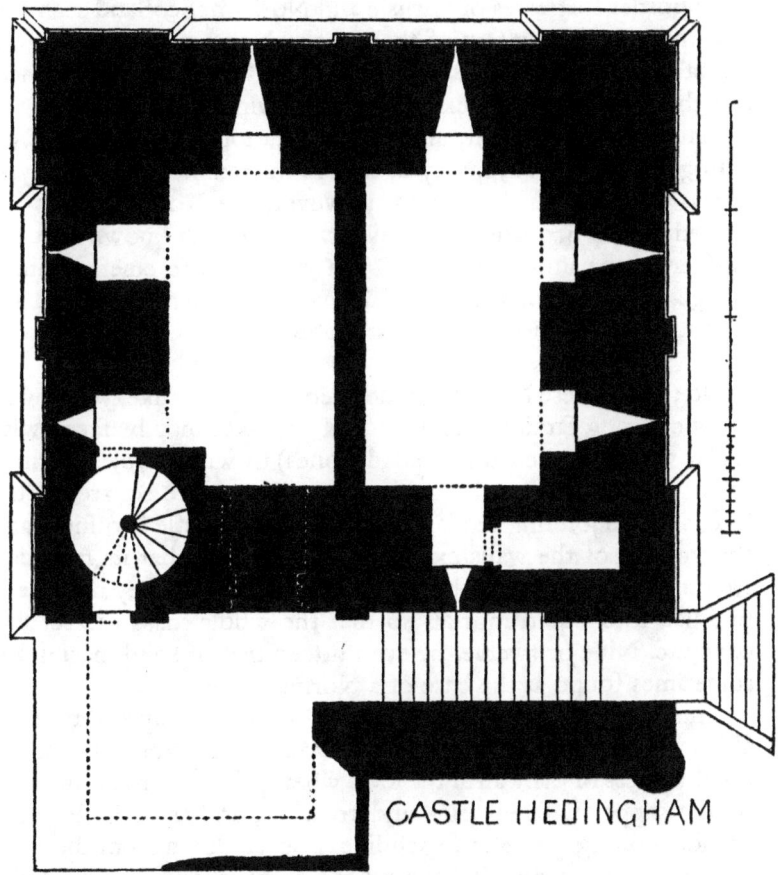

FIG. 2. Hedingham: plan of ground floor.

them. These great stone tower-houses were introduced into Britain by the Normans, and many of them still survive as the familiar 'Norman keeps'. But the stone keep is an exceptional thing, and the vast majority of those Norman barons who came over with the Conqueror housed themselves in timber towers set upon earthen mounds.

GREAT STONE TOWERS AND SHELL-KEEPS

One of the earliest and grandest of Norman keeps is the Tower of London, built by William the Conqueror. Other examples are Colchester; Castle Hedingham in Essex (Fig. 2); Norwich; Newcastle-upon-Tyne; Bamborough in Northumberland; and the great border fortresses of Carlisle and Norham. Scotland seems to have possessed very few of these stone Norman towers, and no doubt most of them were destroyed in the wars of independence. But the remains of one exist at Castle Swin, in Knapdale on the Atlantic coast of Argyll; and the foundations of a small tower, dating from about 1150, may be seen in the remote island of Wyre, in the Orkneys. In those days, however, the Northern Isles belonged not to Scotland but to Norway, and it is known that the builder of the little tower on Wyre was a Norse chief, Kolbein Hruga. After eight centuries his name is still attached to his tower, which is known today as 'Cobbie Row's Castle'.

No two of these Norman stone keeps are quite alike, yet they all show a strong family resemblance. The tower may be faced with ashlar work (squared and dressed stones) or with rubble. Norman ashlar masonry is usually cubical—the stones are square on the face, and the jointing tends to be wide. If the castle is ruined, and the interior of the walls exposed, one will find that its materials have not been laid stone by stone, but are *grouted*; they have been puddled into liquid mortar, so that the whole mass has set like concrete. Nine or twelve, or even fifteen feet of solid masonry is sometimes found at the base of a Norman keep.

This base has often a projecting plinth, or stone apron, running all round the tower. Such a plinth serves two purposes. It adds to the thickness of the wall at the level where it is liable to be attacked by the sapper with his pick and crowbar; and the missiles, firebrands, boiling water and such like, poured down from the summit of the tower, must have bounced or splashed off horizontally to destroy the attacker.

The wall-faces of most of these Norman towers show vertical projecting strips of masonry, known as pilasters. These serve to strengthen the structure. At the four corners, two of these pilasters meet and form a clasping buttress. Often these angle buttresses are large enough to house the spiral stars which ascend the tower, serving each floor in turn and finally conducting to the battle-

GREAT STONE TOWERS AND SHELL-KEEPS

ments. One may usually see from outside that the angle buttress contains a stair, by the series of loopholes or narrow slits which light its winding ascent. In the lower part of the tower the only openings, for reasons of defence, are such narrow slits. These are for air and light, rather than for shooting through. It is impossible to aim effectively through a mere slit in a wall ten feet thick. In the upper parts of the tower, where the living-rooms were, windows may be found. These usually have round arches and zig-zag or other ornament in the Norman manner.

The main entrance to a Norman keep is almost always on the first floor, sometimes even on the second. Generally it was a round-arched door in the Norman style. In the smaller towers, the door would be reached by a wooden ladder, which could be hauled in when danger threatened. The larger towers had a stone forestair, open to the sky, and so completely commanded by the defenders on the wall-head far above. There is a good example at Castle Hedingham (see Fig. 2). In the more elaborate towers, the stair is housed in a forework, and so can be defended by a series of doors or gates, and overlooked by one or more defensive platforms or fighting-decks. There is an excellent example of such a forework at Newcastle-upon-Tyne. In the keep of Dover Castle it is carried round two sides of the tower, so as to form an elaborately defended approach to the entrance.

The battlements of these Norman towers were provided with embrasures, or openings for the archers to shoot through. The solid bit of walling between each pair of embrasures is called a 'merlon'. Sometimes these merlons were pierced with slits for the archer to look through while reloading his crossbow in comparative shelter. In Norman times these parapets were not yet projected forwards on stone brackets, or *corbels*. Where there are such projecting parapets on a Norman keep, it is later, or even modern —as at Newcastle-upon-Tyne. But just below the parapet, in some Norman towers, one may find a row or double row of holes for beams. These supported a timber war-head, which could be added to the tower when preparations were being made to withstand a siege. The Normans called such a timber war-head a *bretasche*: it is the origin of the modern word 'brattice'. Another word for such a timber defence work is a 'hoarding'. It formed a continuous wooden gallery running all round the tower, and enabling the

GREAT STONE TOWERS AND SHELL-KEEPS

garrison to command the assailants at the base, without exposing themselves by leaning out through the stone embrasures. In front of the brattice was a series of loopholes for the archers to shoot through, and in its floor were *meurtrières*, or 'murder holes', through which offensive materials could be cast down upon the attackers. Of course, these timber defences have now all disappeared: but we have pictures of them in old manuscripts. In 1241, such a hoarding was set up, by the King's command, round the top of the Tower of London. It was to be made 'of good strong timber, entirely and well covered with lead, through which people can look even unto the foot of the said tower, and ascend and better defend it, if need be'. (For a picture of hoardings, see Fig. 4.)

The roofs of these Norman keeps were generally fairly steep. In a large tower the roof might be in two spans, with a 'valley' between. In any case the outer walls of the tower would be carried up high, so as to screen the roof from fire-arrows. The result was a great deal of waste space in the top part of the tower. So it came about that later on, when the use of roofing lead became common, the old high-pitched roofs were taken down and a flat leaded platform substituted. In addition to affording an extra storey, this arrangement provided an admirable fighting-deck for the defence of the tower. In Norman keeps there are often signs of this alteration (see Fig. 11): the lines of the original high-pitched roof, and of the flat leaded platform afterwards substitued above it.

The smaller keeps usually have one single room on each floor. In some of the larger ones, such as Rochester (Fig. 3) or Portchester, there is a thick central partition, which may be opened up on the top floors by a handsome arcade of piers and round arches in the Norman style. Some of the larger towers, also, have galleries in the thickness of their walls, both round the tower and traversing the mid-partition, so that the inmates could move freely about without intruding upon the rooms. Much cleverness is shown in the arrangement of the stairs. Frequently a new stair starts from a different point on each floor, so that it was necessary to pass across all the principal rooms, in full view of everybody, to reach the summit of the keep. Most Norman keeps have a well inside them, but few have a separate kitchen. Meals were prepared in peacetime in a wooden kitchen inside the courtyard. At a pinch, the fireplaces in the principal rooms of the tower could be used

FIG. 3. Rochester: interior view of keep.

GREAT STONE TOWERS AND SHELL-KEEPS

for emergency cooking. These fireplaces discharged their smoke by means of flues in the walls, not carried up into chimneys, but venting through the outer faces. The fireplaces are usually inadequate, and Norman keeps must have been extremely cold. Small closets or bedrooms were provided in the thickness of the walls: in some of the larger keeps like Dover or Newcastle, this provision is quite elaborate. There were also privies, which discharged by shafts carried down through the thickness of the outer walls. Many of the bigger keeps have an oratory, sometimes quite a large and ornate chapel. A good example may be seen in the keep of Newcastle. By far the largest example is the Chapel of St. John in the Tower of London. This forms a semi-circular apse projecting from the east face of the tower. The great keep of Colchester Castle, the largest in area in England, is arranged on the same plan. This mighty tower is remarkable because it is mostly built out of stones and brick taken from the Roman town of *Camulodunum*.

Some of the rooms, especially the smaller ones in a Norman keep, are gloomily vaulted in stone; but sometimes the vaulting has been put in later. For example, the great vault which spans the keep at Newcastle, under the roof, is entirely modern. At Carlisle a vault in the same position was inserted during the reign of Queen Elizabeth, so as to provide a platform for mounting guns on top of the keep.

It is wrong to imagine that these vaults were all dungeons, in which captives languished in misery or suffered hideous torments, such as Front-de-Boeuf proposed to inflict upon Isaac the Jew. The vaults in an ancient castle were not normally used for any such horrible purpose. They were for storage. In the Middle Ages every household had to be more or less self-supporting. So the castle had to provide storage for large quantities of meal, casks of salted fish, whole carcases of beef and mutton, barrels of ale and foreign wine, and what not. It was for this purpose that the great vaults were provided. Where there is a dungeon or 'pit', it is usually quite small, and is often, though not always, provided with a latrine. Frequently the only access to such a prison is by a trap-door in the floor above.

Dark and cheerless abodes, smoky and draughty and smelly these keeps must have been, by our standards. Perhaps they were

GREAT STONE TOWERS AND SHELL-KEEPS

not quite so gloomy inside as we now find them, for the walls were partly covered with bright-coloured tapestries, and, where bare, were often whitewashed, both outside and inside. The Tower of London was called 'the White Tower' for this reason. The keep of Corfe Castle in Dorset is also known to have been whitewashed. The floors were strewn with rushes or herbs: the furniture was massive and scanty.

In the same way as, from an early date, there were some stone towers alongside the tower-houses of wood, so also in some cases the palisading round the summit of a *motte* was soon replaced by a ring wall of stone. In this way arose the kind of castle which has been called a shell-keep. Good examples may be seen at Carisbrooke in the Isle of Wight; Tonbridge in Kent; in the Castle of Lincoln; at Tickhill in Yorkshire; and at Tamworth in Staffordshire, the ancient stronghold of the Marmions. In Cornwall there is a remarkable group of shell-keeps, of which perhaps the masterpiece is Restormel. Here, as at Tamworth, the interior of the shell-keep is now crowded with later buildings.

Most of the great stone tower-houses in England were not erected before the twelfth century. On the other hand it seems that the fashion of building shell-keeps began rather earlier. So it comes about that in a number of these shell-keeps masonry is found which is older than most tower-houses. Sometimes this masonry shows a very remarkable style of construction known as herring-bone work. The courses of stone are laid slantwise, and in each course they slope in the opposite direction from the courses above and below. It is believed that all such herring-bone work is older than about the year 1100. There is a conspicuous example of it at Tamworth Castle. Much of the inner walling of Colchester Castle, a very early tower, is built in herring-bone work. At Corfe Castle there survives a fragment of an early hall built in this way.

In Plate 1 some Norman herring-bone masonry is seen added on top of a Roman tower at Pevensey Castle.

IV
How Castles were Attacked and Defended

IF, as was often the case, the town walls, or the outer defences of the castle, were enclosed by a moat—a ditch full of water—the first task before the besiegers was to fill this up. This they attempted to do by throwing in bundles of faggots, or baskets filled with earth. The defenders would seek to kill or disable as many as they could of the labourers as they ran forward with their loads to the edge of the moat. To protect these poor wretches, the attackers in their turn would endeavour with their arrows and slingstones to drive the defenders off their wall-heads. For this purpose, the archers and slingers would advance under the protection of movable wooden shields called *pavises*, which could be wheeled forward against the castle, protecting the archer while he reloaded his bow and searched for a target. The pavise therefore had a slit in it to enable the man behind to keep a look-out. You will see these pavises in Fig. 4.

In the attack and defence of fortified places, the weapon used was the crossbow rather than the longbow. The crossbow was mounted horizontally upon a stock, and fired from the shoulder by a trigger, like a modern gun. The bow itself was often made of horn. It was so powerful that the string could not be pulled back by hand, as with a longbow, but had to be cranked up with a small windlass that could be attached to the stock. To enable the archer to do this better, a stirrup was sometimes provided at the front end of the bow. The crossbow discharged a short arrow known as a 'quarrel' or more simply as a 'bolt'. Its point was shaped like a long pyramid, with three edges instead of the two edges

FIG. 4. Siege of a castle, showing the use of a 'belfy', a 'cat' and 'pavises' and catapults. Note the brattice or hoarding on the round tower.

of the ordinary arrow point. Thus it had tremendous smashing power, and was able to penetrate the chain mail of the time. The effective range of the English longbow was 220 yards, but that of the crossbow was no less than 340 yards, and even longer shots are on record. On the other hand, compared with the longbow the crossbow was clumsy and slow. It is said of the English archers that they had three arrows in use at any given moment: one was striking its mark, the second was in mid-air, and the third was leaving the bow! So it came about that the English archers easily overwhelmed the French crossbowmen at such battles as Crécy and Agincourt. But in the attack and defence of fortified places, where the crossbowman worked behind shelter, the superior strength of his weapon told. The bow-slits in the towers of an ancient castle open behind into quite large wall-chambers, with space enough for two men, or at least for a man and a boy. In each stood a skilled crossbowman, and behind him a lad with a spare bow, ready loaded, so that a continuous discharge could be kept up. In just the same way in a modern grouse drive, when the birds are coming over thick and fast, the sportsman in his butt has a loader with a spare gun beside him. In the big castles built by Edward I to hold down Wales—Conway and Caernarvon and the others—such a system may be clearly seen; and there were long galleries in the thickness of the walls so that the archers could move quickly from point to point.

Where the walls of the castle were garnished by timber war-heads—the brattices or hoardings mentioned above—the assailants would endeavour to set these ablaze by fire-arrows, or with fire-pots hurled by their catapults, which could also cast up great stones. These catapults, or spring-guns, were very ingenious constructions, sometimes of great size, requiring many men to work them, and capable of casting large stones to a long distance. Fig. 4 is a picture showing some of these contraptions in action.

Suppose now that the besiegers have succeeded in driving the defenders from their wall-heads, or at least in so overmastering their counter-fire as to be able to fill up the ditch. They are now in a position to attack the castle wall at close quarters. This could be done in four ways: by using a battering-ram; by sapping through the wall with pickaxes and crowbars; by undermining; or by the use of a 'belfry' (Fig. 5). A belfry was a tall wooden tower, several

FIG. 5. Attack on a castle with a 'belfry'.

HOW CASTLES WERE ATTACKED AND DEFENDED

storeys high so as to overtop the walls. At the summit was a drawbridge. The whole thing ran on wheels, and was pushed forward against the wall over the filled-up ditch. Those who had filled in the ditch would previously have laid across the pile a road of logs—a corduroy road we should call it nowadays—sloping down towards the castle, so that the belfry when once wheeled on to the roadway would run down and attach itself to the wall by its own momentum. The timber-work of the belfry would be covered with hides drenched in water to protect it against fire. As soon as it had reached the wall the attackers would drop their drawbridge on to the parapet, swarm across, fight their way out on either side along the ramparts, and thus seek to gain possession of the stairs leading down to the interior of the castle or town.

In the famous siege of Kenilworth Castle by Henry III in 1265, no less than eleven great catapults were plied against the walls. Some of their stone balls, 18 inches in diameter, have been found among the ruins. King Henry constructed two belfries or wooden towers, one of which was large enough to contain two hundred men. The water defences of the castle prevented the use of mines, and in the end the place was forced to yield only by famine and disease. The garrison was reduced to eating its horses, and when at length the besiegers entered the castle there was a fearful stench of dead men and animals.

In September 1301, when Edward I besieged Bothwell Castle (Fig. 15)—one of the largest and strongest of Scottish castles —he used a belfry. This engine was built in Glasgow, nine miles away, and detailed payments are recorded to the carpenters, plumbers and other workmen, and for buying the lead, wheels, cables, wax, and other materials used in its construction and working. No less than thirty wagons were required to transport the cumbrous engine to Bothwell, and the journey took two days. A bridge was built to bring the belfry across the Clyde, and a corduroy road was laid from the bridge up to the castle.

If the attackers decided to use one of the other methods mentioned, a different approach was necessary. They would then construct what was called a 'cat' or a 'sow'. This was a wooden penthouse, so strongly framed that it could resist the stones dropped down upon it, and covered with drenched skins to protect it from fire. It was wheeled against the base of the wall, and under its

HOW CASTLES WERE ATTACKED AND DEFENDED

shelter the assailants would seek to beat the wall in with a battering-ram, or to dig their way through it with axe and crowbar. In 1230 the Norsemen broke into Rothesay Castle in this way.

Where the state of the ground permitted, the assailants might employ a mine. This was the most dangerous form of attack. An underground tunnel was driven beneath the wall, its roof being supported on timber props, like the pit-props used in coal-mines today. When the tunnel had reached the requisite length, its further end was packed with combustibles. These were then fired, and the miners hurriedly withdrew. The fire burnt through the props, the roof of the gallery fell in, and the wall above, of course, collapsed. Into the breach the assailants rushed, clambering over fallen masonry and seeking to overwhelm the defenders stunned by the crash. At St. Andrews Castle we may still see such a mine gallery, as well as a counter-mine made by the besieged. These were made during the famous siege of this castle in 1546. Hearing the approach of the sappers by the noise of their tools underground, the defenders ran out a counter-mine towards the sound, broke into the mine and, after an underground struggle, killed the attacking miners or drove them out.

When attacking the walls by battering-ram or sap, the assailants would seek to attach themselves to an angle. Here the corner stones could be more easily dislodged. In the same way, a mine driven under an angle would be likely to bring down two lengths of wall and thus open a wider breach. In 1215 John overthrew a corner of Rochester Castle in this way. The repair to the castle can still be seen, and a round bastion was built instead of the old square corner, so as to get rid of the angle, which is always the weak point in a rectangular tower.

Of course in suitable cases, instead of proceeding by way of regular siege, the attackers might endeavour to storm the castle at once by beating in the gates. Usually, however, it was easier to win the gate by stratagem than by open force, as at Linlithgow Castle which was won thus from its English garrison. Under cover of a truce a cart-load of hay was driven under the portal, with armed men concealed in the hay. The cart was halted under the portcullis, so that the latter could not be let down; the Scots sprang out of the hay, slew the porters and admitted their friends. A portcullis was a great gate of iron, or of wood shod with iron,

HOW CASTLES WERE ATTACKED AND DEFENDED

which could be let down through a slot in the vaulting of the entrance passage. It was usually placed inside the wooden doors, so that if these were burnt or broken up, the portcullis behind, which could not be so easily destroyed, would hold, and the defenders could shoot out between its intersecting bars. In addition to the defences, the entrance passage would be pierced above with 'murder holes', through which the garrison overhead could hurl down offensive materials on those who strove to fight their way in.

In the more important castles, the gateway was often still further defended by a *barbican*. This was a kind of fortified outwork, often on the other side of the moat. At the siege of Torquilstone in *Ivanhoe*, it was such an outwork which was the first part of the castle to be attacked and stormed by the Black Knight and his stout comrades of the greenwood. Sir Walter Scott thus describes the Norman barbican at Torquilstone:

'It was an extensive fortification of no great height or strength, intended to protect the postern gate through which Cedric had been recently dismissed by Front-de-Boeuf. The castle moat divided this species of barbican from the rest of the fortress, so that, in case of its being taken, it was easy to cut off the communication with the main building, by withdrawing the temporary bridge. In the outwork was a sally-port corresponding to the postern of the castle, and the whole was surrounded by a strong palisade.'[1]

In the thirteenth century, such a barbican, particularly if in advance of the main entry of the castle, was often a very formidable structure. One of the largest and best preserved in England is the Black Gate at the castle of Newcastle-upon-Tyne. This was built by Henry III, and the work was started in 1247, for a total cost of £547 15s. 11d. The Black Gate consists of two D-shaped towers set back to back on each side of a portal, behind which is an entrance passage, defended by a drawbridge over an outer ditch, a portcullis, and folding gates, as well as by a murder hole opening in the vault above. This barbican stands beyond the main ditch of the castle, and is so placed as to flank or enfilade it. This means that the archers in the barbican could sweep with their fire the whole length of the ditch. To enable them to do so, the

[1] *Ivanhoe*, Chap. XXIX.

HOW CASTLES WERE ATTACKED AND DEFENDED

barbican is swung round at an angle to the castle front. In this way a further advantage is secured to the defenders, for the passage through the barbican, and across the ditch to the inner or main gate of the castle, has to be a bent one; and this could check a direct inward rush of the assailants if they succeeded in carrying the barbican gate.

If the castle was a small one, with no moat and not too high, the enemy might try to climb into it with scaling-ladders. There is a curious account of how, in the siege of a Scotch tower, such an attempt was foiled by a very simple device. All round the top of the walls the defenders hung a series of heavy wooden beams. When the assailants under cover of night set their ladders against the walls, the alert garrison cut the ropes supporting the beams: and down they fell, hurling ladders and attackers to the ground.

All castles were designed for defence, and are rightly regarded as examples of military architecture; but foremost the castle is a landowner's residence, although in those unquiet times it had to be fortified. People tend to think of ancient castles as if they were always armed and fully manned—the men-at-arms all at their action stations, spring-guns cocked, sentries alert and watchful on the battlements; but no ancient castle, even on the war-torn Borders, was ever maintained in anything like a state of instant and anxious readiness. On the contrary, the evidence is ample that even the most important castles, especially when the lord was not in residence, were usually kept up on a care-and-maintenance basis. The garrison might consist of no more than porter, a housekeeper, and one or two domestics. And even when the lord was there, the castle was not stuffed with mail-clad men-at-arms. Its inmates were the baron's household—his family and their servants. In war his castle would be guarded by his tenantry who dwelt around, and who, in such an emergency, would be called upon to do their feudal military service. In the case of a great lord's castle, some of his senior vassals might be liable, in time of need, thus to provide the garrison for a particular tower. Sometimes, as at Dover Castle, some of the towers are still called by the names of those who had to defend them in this way. This was called 'tenure by castle guard'. It will be seen how in the later Middle Ages all this was changed by rapid advances in the art of war.

V
Exploring a Norman Castle

I PROPOSE to take the royal castle of Newcastle-upon-Tyne as a particular example which may be explored in some detail. It has one of the finest and best-preserved Norman keeps in the country. Also as it was a royal castle, there are building and other expense accounts, as well as other information about it, preserved in the public records, which help to the understanding of its interior arrangements.

In Figs. 7–11 there are plans of all the floors, as well as a section showing the tower as if it had been sliced down from east to west, and the north half removed, so that one looks into the southern half.

Newcastle-upon-Tyne began its life as a Roman town. It grew up under the shelter of one of the forts or stations on the Great Wall of Hadrian. The name the Romans gave it was *Pons Aelius*. Some years ago, Roman foundations were unearthed close beside the Norman keep. It is therefore probable that the Roman fort stood more or less where the castle now stands.

After the Roman soldiers left, the Angles settled on Tyneside: and, a little later, within the walls of the abandoned Roman fort a brotherhood of Christian monks took up their abode. So the old English gave the place the name of *Monkchester*.

William the Conqueror's eldest son, Robert Curthose, Duke of Normandy, planted a Norman castle in 1080 on the old site of the Roman Pons Aelius and the Anglian Monkchester. He was nicknamed Curthose because of his short legs. Being a new foundation, his castle was called the Newcastle-upon-Tyne, and this name came to be given to the town which grew up under the protection of the Norman stronghold.

Duke Robert's castle was made of earthwork and timber on the mount-and-bailey plan (Fig. 6). The site of its mount can still be traced in what is now called the Half-Moon Battery, at the east

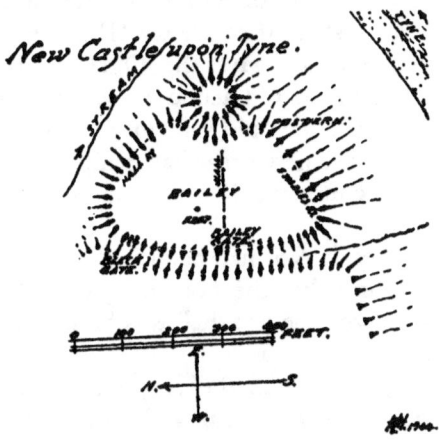

FIG. 6. Newcastle-upon-Tyne: plan of Norman earthwork castle

end of the castle bailey—though practically all the earthwork has now disappeared. In course of time the palisades of the early castle were as usual replaced by stone walling. Bits of these walls still remain, including a fine Norman postern on the south side, leading out towards the Tyne. King John seems to have built a shell wall, with many buttresses, round the top of the *motte*. Old pictures still preserve the appearance of this shell-keep. Like the *mottes* at Tamworth, Tonbridge, and Windsor, this at Newcastle contained a well.

Before that time King Henry II had built the mighty square keep which is still the glory of Newcastle. The public accounts show that the work was begun in 1172 and finished in 1177. Its total cost was £911 10s. 9d.—of course a very large sum for those days. The architect's name was Maurice; and he it was who, ten years later, built a second great Norman keep at Dover Castle, which has many resemblances to the keep at Newcastle.

EXPLORING A NORMAN CASTLE

After King John had built his shell-keep on top of the *motte*, his father's square keep became known as the 'Old Tower'.

The next important building to be erected in the castle was the great hall on the east side of the bailey. This was the work of Henry III, and the accounts show that it was going up in 1237. Nothing of this hall now remains above ground. Its site is partly occupied by the County Council buildings. But it appears that there was also an earlier hall on a different site, doubtless belonging to the Norman castle. After Henry III's new hall was built, this Norman hall became known as the 'Old Hall'. It had a chamber attached to it. Thus in the old accounts we have 'the king's old hall with its chamber', the 'old hall in the old Tower', that is Henry II's keep, and the new great hall built by Henry III. These old records can be confusing if one looks only at the existing remains.

I suspect that the early Norman hall lay along the straight south side of the bailey, and that the postern gate had to do with it. This would explain why the new hall was built, less conveniently, on the east side.

Finally, in 1247, was begun the very fine barbican, the Black Gate. Like the keep, this has fortunately come down in excellent preservation (see p. 26).

Looking at the keep (Plate 2) one notices that it has the usual broad-spreading plinth or base, tall buttresses, and projecting corner turrets: but the north-west turret is multangular in shape, instead of square like the others. This was probably so as to provide room on top for a small catapult, as this corner, and the west front, were the most exposed quarters of the keep, and indeed of the whole castle.[1] The buttress in the middle of the west front is bigger than the others, because it contains the shafts of the latrines; and at the foot of the buttress is a door, so that the soil-pit could be cleared out. These conveniences were placed on the side of the tower away from the courtyard, so that the refuse from them could easily be drained or carried off into the castle ditch.

The doors and windows of the keep are all round-arched and ornamented in the Norman style. But the masonry is not typical

[1] There is a model of one of these catapults in the museum now housed inside the castle.

of a Norman castle; instead of being square-faced, the stones are long and low in the course. This was a new style of building which became general in the thirteenth century, and shows that the Newcastle keep is a very late one of its kind.

For more than a century railway trains have passed and repassed Henry II's keep, smothering it in their smoke: so that now, like the great tower of the castle of Plessis-les-Tours, as described by Sir Walter Scott in *Quentin Durward*, it 'rises, like a black Ethiopian giant, high into the air'.[1] But the days of the steam locomotive are numbered, and perhaps the time is now not long distant when the successive blasts of smoke will be no more. Then the Town Council of Newcastle will be able to clean its walls and to restore to their venerable stronghold the beautiful golden colour of its Northumbrian freestone.

On the east front of the keep is a forework. This is an elaborate affair. Once it had three towers, but only the middle and upper towers now remain. A flight of steps leads up to a portal in the middle tower. On the right is the long slot into which the drawbar was pushed back when the gate was opened. Inside, the stair continues upwards under a vaulted passage with sloping roof. On either side is a little niche with a basin for oil and a wick, to serve as a lamp.

At the top of the stair (Fig. 7) is a platform. On the left side, and up a short flight of steps, is the main door into the keep—a fine Norman portal, though its stonework has been renewed. It enters the keep on the second floor, that is, at the third storey; an arrangement which dictated the whole plan of the interior of the keep. Such a high entrance, reached by an exposed outer stair defended by three towers, added greatly to the strength of the place. Apart from the well-secured passages by which the stair had to pass through the two lower towers, it would be commanded by the defenders on the flat roofs of all three towers, as well as from the parapet on the summit of the keep itself.

In front of the stair landing, a door leads into a room in the third and uppermost tower. This room has been restored, but on the old lines. It is a handsome apartment with a good fireplace, and clearly was meant to serve as an important living-room. We can hardly doubt that this was the constable's lodging when the

[1] *Quentin Durward*, Chap. III.

King was in residence, controlling the whole stair of approach and the entrance into the royal apartments. The constable must have sat here as the King's representative, interviewing callers who

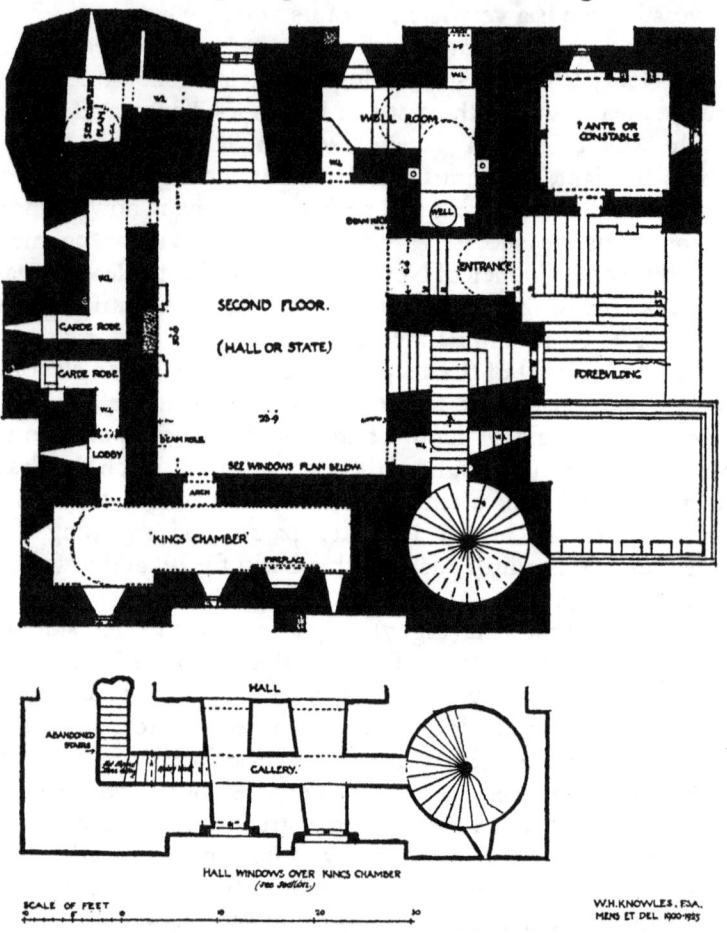

FIG. 7. Newcastle-upon-Tyne: plan of keep at second-floor level.

wanted an audience with the sovereign, hearing suits on the King's behalf and dealing out justice. It is appropriate that this room should now be used as the office of the Warden of the keep.

The main door into the keep leads into a large room which occupied the whole of the second floor. Today, this room is very

1. Pevensey Castle, The Roman wall and towers. Note the Norman herring bone masonry on top

(See pp. 19, 45, 142-6)

2. The Keep of the Castle of Newcastle-upon-Tyne
(See pp. 28-41)

lofty, and covered over by a dark vault; but this vault is modern. In the side walls near the top of the room are marks showing that there was once another storey overhead, with a high-pitched roof which was concealed by the lofty walls and battlements. There is also evidence that this roof has at one time been heightened. Last of all the roof was removed and a flat leaded platform substituted. Such traces are often found in Norman keeps.

This great room was the King's Hall. It is well lit, with a fireplace on the west side. At the lower or north end, to the right of the entrance, a door leads into a vaulted room in which is a well. On either side of the well is a recess for keeping a bucket, and in the sills of each recess a hole. Into these water could be poured, which was carried down by pipes into the cellar of the tower, and also into a cistern provided for the use of the lowest of the three towers of the forework. The well is 99 feet in depth, and still contains about 50 feet of water. From this room another door opens in the outside wall. At present this door gives access to nothing but mid-air: but it is certain that there was here a timber annexe outside, bracketed on to the wall, and doubtless containing a fireplace or cooking stance—so that this room, with a water supply available from the well, formed the King's kitchen.

Also at the lower end of the hall, opposite the entrance, there opens a closet in the thickness of the wall. This contains a privy.

In the upper left-hand or south end wall of the hall a door leads into the King's Chamber. This is quite a large room, vaulted, of course, as it is hollowed out in the thickness of the wall. It is amply lit, and has a large handsome fireplace. Three of the windows on the south side would give pleasant glimpses of the Tyne. From the fourth window, in the west wall, the king could look out on the town. Opening off the lower end of the chamber is a privy. In a record of 1237, this apartment is described as 'the King's Chamber in the Old Tower'.

It was explained in Chapter III that the usual arrangement of a house in the Middle Ages comprised a central hall, with the kitchen at the lower end and the lord's private room, or solar, at the upper; and that a tower-house is really such a hall-house up-ended for reasons of safety. But here in this large royal tower the King's Hall has its kitchen at the lower end and its solar at the upper, all on the same flat as in an ordinary dwelling of the time. It is easy to understand how much more convenient this arrangement was.

One other thing should be noticed in the King's Hall. From a window at its lower, that is its right-hand or north side, opens a vaulted prison in the north-west turret of the keep. The door closes against the prison, secured by a drawbar.

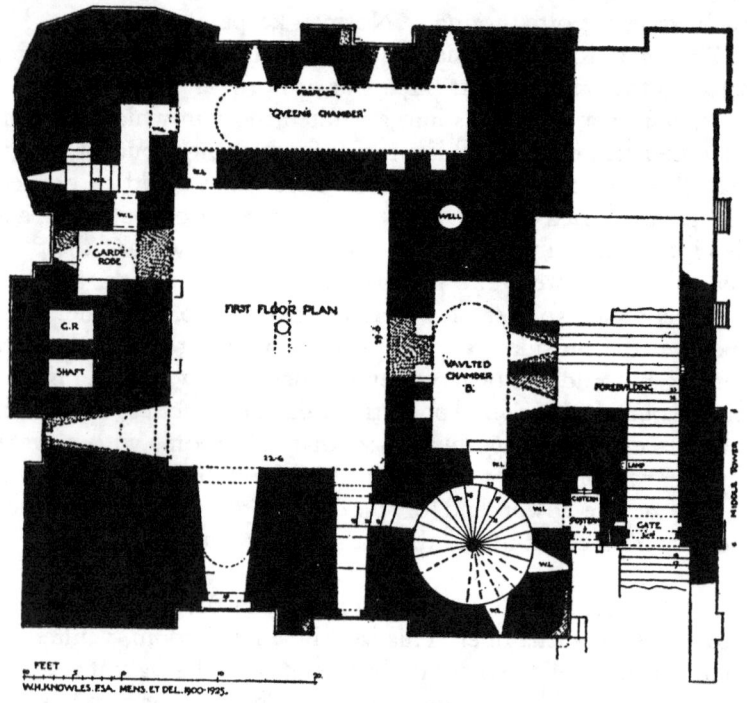

FIG. 8. Newcastle-upon-Tyne: plan of keep at first-floor level.

At the south-east corner of the King's Hall a door opens to the main stair of the keep. This is of the corkscrew pattern, and descends in a continuous easy spiral right down to the bottom of the tower, as well as winding upwards to the storey above the King's Hall and then to the parapets. The lobby outside the door from the King's Hall is lit by a loophole during day-time, and there is a nook for a lamp at night.

At the level of the first floor (Fig. 8) is the Queen's Hall corresponding to the King's Hall overhead, with the Queen's Chamber adjoining it in just the same way. Only in this case the Queen's Chamber is at the north, not the south end of her hall. It is, however, still in its proper place, opening off the *upper* end of the hall: for the Queen's Hall is entered at the *south*-east corner, from the spiral stair, whereas the King's Hall on the floor above is entered at the *north*-east corner, by the main outer portal of the tower.

One sees from this how well-thought-out the whole plan of the tower is. Another advantage of the alternate position of the King's and the Queen's Chambers is that by placing them so, the architect avoided having to hollow out both these large rooms in the same wall. Two such chambers made in the same wall, one above the other, would have greatly weakened the structure. Maurice, the royal architect, knew his job.

The Queen's Hall is fitted up very similarly to the King's. It has its fireplace, good windows and a privy. The pillar and the two arches, however, are modern. So also the Queen's Chamber closely resembles the King's. But, unlike the King's Chamber, it has two small lockers or wall-presses. At the lower end of the Queen's Chamber, a door admits to a passage communicating with the hall privy, and also to a narrow stair which descends in the multangular turret, to a vaulted cellar immediately underneath the Queen's Chamber.

It is easy to understand why the Queen's apartments have been placed below the King's. The royal lady and her attendants had to be given the utmost privacy. Therefore they would never have been placed at the entrance level, with the outer door of the keep opening directly into them. But as the entrance door in this tower is placed on the *second* floor, the King's apartments had to be here; and therefore, because the top flat was required (as we shall see) for the garrison, the Queen's apartments had to be below those of the King. This is really an inversion of what we should have expected: and it is all due to the fact that in this keep the main entrance, for security reasons, has been placed on the second floor. As the plan is arranged, nobody can reach the Queen's rooms without first passing through the King's.

In 1251 Henry III gave orders to build a house for himself and his Queen at Freemantle in Hampshire. The house was to contain a hall, a kitchen and a chamber with an upper storey, and a chapel on the ground floor, all for the King's use, and a chamber with an upper storey, with a chapel at the end of the same chamber, for the Queen's use. Under the chamber was to be made a cellar for the King's wines.

So it was customary for the royal couple to have separate apartments, and the kind of accommodation needed was much the same as that provided in the keep at Newcastle-upon-Tyne. At Freemantle the King's wine cellar was to be placed below the Queen's Chamber—in the most secure and private place that could be found for it. This is just the position of the vaulted cellar below the Queen's Chamber at Newcastle. More than likely, therefore, when the court was in residence the royal wine was kept here.

One other thing remains to be mentioned before leaving the first-floor plan of the keep. Opening off the main stair, between the Queen's Hall and the forework, is a vaulted closet, containing three lockers. It has no fireplace, and was originally lit only by two narrow slits. Probably this was a store-room. The slits have now been widened and a door broken through into the Queen's Hall.

Down the great winding stair, at the ground floor or basement of the tower (Fig. 9), we find a large vaulted cellar, fireproof and dry, well suited for keeping an ample supply of provisions. The vaulting rests on eight stout semi-circular ribs which spring from a fine Norman pillar. In the south-west corner is a prison, with a privy. One imagines that the more common sort of prisoners were kept here, while people of greater importance would be put into the upper prison beside the King's Hall. There is also, at ground level, another large vaulted store-room between the main building and the forework, in the same position as the one above.

There is a very interesting window on the south side of this cellar. A window of some sort was necessary to give light to those working in the cellar. But as it is near ground level, there was a danger of arrows, perhaps fire-arrows, being shot in. So the rear arch which spans the inner end of the deep bay made by the window in the thick wall is kept low, so that an arrow shot in would rebound from a solid plate of wall, and could not possibly reach the cellar.

In later days a postern door was opened at ground level on the west side of the keep. This would be useful for getting in stores, which previously must have had to be carried right up the forestair to the portal on the second floor, and then down the spiral stair again to the cellar in the basement. Still later, a second postern was made in the south wall. Of course these posterns could somewhat weaken the security of the keep. But in all the old castles there was a constant tug-of-war between safety and convenience. When convenience had entirely won, the day of castles was over.

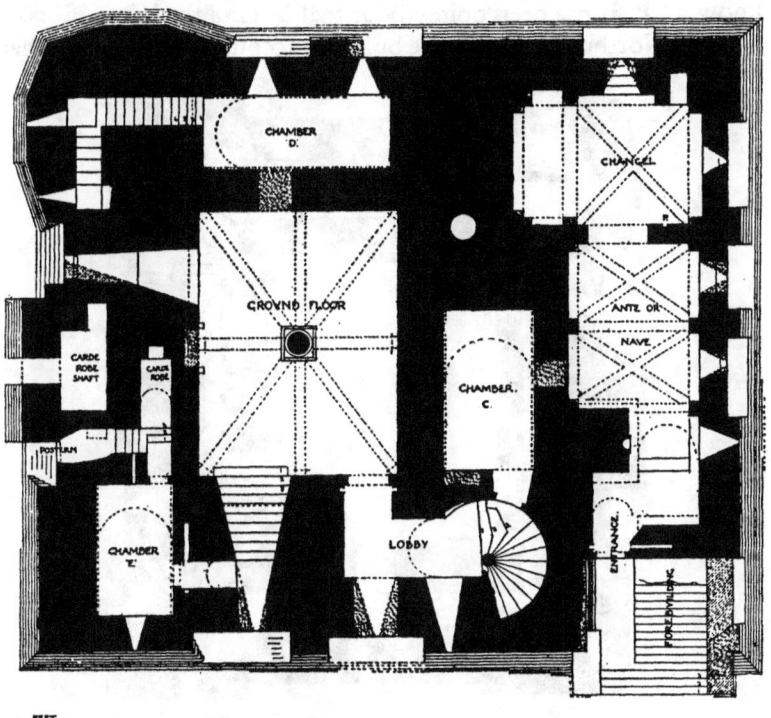

FIG. 9. Newcastle-upon-Tyne: plan of keep at ground-floor level.

The great central pillar of the cellar (Fig. 11) is hollow. Into it water was conducted by pipes from the castle well, and there used to be a tap at its base. So those working in the cellar were provided with a water supply.

A flight of steps starts at the entrance from the main spiral stair to the King's Hall, mounting north in the east wall. A little higher up the main stair, a passage leads out in the thickness of the south wall of the tower (see the lower plan in Fig. 7). This passage passes through the bays of the two windows of the King's Hall, turns the corner in the south-west turret, and then becomes a stair, which mounts up a little distance in the west wall, and then stops in solid masonry.

Clearly there has been a change of plan here, but we do not know what. It has been pointed out that in 1174 the King of Scots invaded Northumberland. The building accounts show that in that

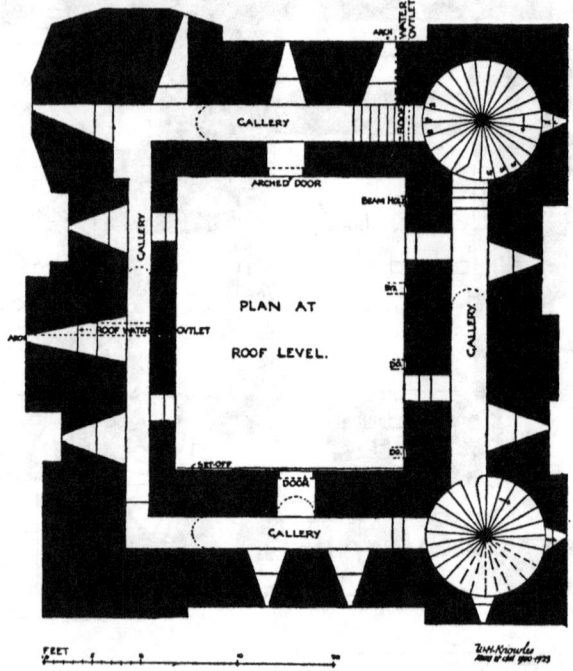

FIG. 10. Newcastle-upon-Tyne: plan of keep at roof level.

year work on the tower at Newcastle almost came to a standstill. Possibly, when it was resumed, the design may have been changed.

In the upper part of the King's Hall (Fig. 10) a vaulted gallery runs all round inside the four walls of the tower. There are external loop-holes, and on all four sides doors lead into the topmost flat of the tower, though there is no floor here now. And at its northeast corner this passage gives access to a *second* spiral stair, in the square turret which caps this angle. This stair leads up to the battlements, and also down to meet the straight stair which ascends in the east wall from near the door of the King's Hall.

The topmost flat was of course set aside for the garrison—a small number of picked men—so that they would be available promptly to man the fighting-deck on top of the tower. 'To the walls!' cries the Templar in the siege of Torquilstone; for in these Norman keeps the principal defence was always conducted from the flat roof and the battlements. Studying the plans and the section, one realizes how ingenious is the arrangement of the tower at this level. The passage in the thickness of the wall would allow the soldiers to move all round the tower, and by means of the two spiral stairs to gain the battlements and reinforce them at whatever point they were threatened. Using the passage in this way they would not need to move all round the wall-walk itself, and so would not get into the way of those already defending it. Nor would they have to cross the garrison hall, which in time of siege would doubtless be cumbered with military stores.

Before the uppermost storey and flat roof were raised, the men-at-arms must have been lodged in a garret under the original high-pitched roof. It will be remembered that the marks of two successive such ridge-roofs remain on the north and south walls of the keep (see Fig. 11). We know from the records that in 1240 the roof was given a covering of lead, and this may therefore be the time when the old ridged roof was taken down and a flat fighting-deck put in its place. By this period light catapults were in general use for the defence of castles, and so the towers were often provided with flat roofs for mounting them. Sometimes the lead of such roofs was laid upon a bed of sand, so as to make the roof fireproof.

By now the meaning of the straight stair in the east wall, connecting the main spiral stair in the south-eastern turret with the second spiral stair in the turret at the north-east corner, will be clear. This latter stair starts from the third floor only, whereas the main stair ascends the whole height of the tower. If the forebuilding were captured and the main entrance to the tower mastered by the assailants, so that they had thus gained entrance to the King's Hall, the garrison on the flat above and on their wall-heads would not be trapped. They could descend by the north-east turret stair and by the straight flight of steps in the east wall, and escape down the main stair in the south-east turret. If still full of fight, they could invade the King's Hall by its south-east door. If not, a way of escape was provided for them by a postern door which gave access from the main stair at the first-floor level, by

FIG. 11. Newcastle-upon-Tyne: section through keep looking south.

means of a flying bridge, on to the top of the lowest of the three forework towers. This tower has now gone, but the postern and the corbels or stone brackets for the bridge, high up on the face of the middle tower, can still be seen (Fig. 8). Both in this tower

EXPLORING A NORMAN CASTLE

and in the basement of the keep, they would still have water available. Everything had been well thought out.

One important room of the fascinating keep remains to be described. At the foot of the forestair, almost hidden between the forework and the main building, a small door leads into a lovely Norman chapel (see Fig. 9) placed under the ascending stair and towers of the forework. This chapel, having an independent outside entrance and (originally) no internal access from the keep, must obviously have been intended to serve the general household in the castle as well as the royal personages and their attendants in the keep.

Visiting the keep at Newcastle in these days, one is struck by the darkness of its interiors. No doubt these great Norman towers were always somewhat gloomy abodes, but at Newcastle one should remember that the interiors, like the outside, are encrusted with more than a century of railway and industrial soot. Moreover, the museum cases and exhibits with which the rooms are filled of course increase the darkness. Originally the walls were plastered, and would be whitewashed, or, in the state rooms, painted with bright colours.

VI
Courtyard Castles and Fortified Manor-houses

THE result of contact, during the Crusades, with the civilization of the East was that the Crusaders learned many useful arts and crafts, which they brought back with them. In particular, the science of fortification, the arts of attack and defence, were understood and practised with far greater elaboration and skill by the ingenious Byzantines and Saracens than by the rough feudal knighthood of Britain or France. But the Western knights, if not so civilized, were quick to learn. So the lessons taught, often at cruel cost, in the siege or defence of the strong cities and castles of the East, were put to good use when the Crusaders returned to their own countries. The result was a great and rapid advance in the art of castle building in France and England during the Crusading period—that is, in the twelfth and thirteenth centuries.

In the Norman stone castles the principal feature, as we have seen, was the rectangular tower or keep. If there was a stone curtain wall attached to it, this was, in general, a subordinate feature. Apart from the way in which it could be defended from the wall-heads, the chief strength of the Norman keep lay in the solidity of its masonry. In other words, its capacity for resistance was in the main a passive one. If well provisioned and well equipped, the garrison could sit tight within their massive walls. Supposing that they had found time to sweep the countryside around clear of provisions, it might well be that their assailants would starve in their lines before the castle, while the besieged still had ample supplies. An English army besieging Dirleton Castle, near Edin-

COURTYARD CASTLES AND FORTIFIED MANOR-HOUSES

burgh, in 1298, nearly came to grief in this way. They were reduced to eating beans gleaned in the fields, when by good luck a ship laden with provisions arrived in the Firth of Forth. On the other hand, if the besiegers were well provisioned, they needed only to blockade the castle, and sooner or later it must fall. It therefore became a prime concern of the defenders to plan their castle for a defence so active and so aggressive that the assailants could not maintain themselves before its walls, and might then be driven to raise the siege. This very nearly happened at the siege of Kildrummy Castle in Aberdeenshire in 1306. The English assailants, under Prince Edward of Caernarvon (afterwards Edward II), were almost driven from their lines by the active defenders, and were on the point of abandoning the siege, when a traitor set the castle on fire.

The principal way in which the desire for a more aggressive defence was accomplished was by increasing the importance of the curtain wall. It was built larger, thicker, and loftier, to withstand the more powerful siege engines and the taller 'belfries' which the military men of the West had learned to construct in the Crusades. Moreover, a much more active defence was provided by placing, at frequent intervals along the curtain walls, and specially at the corners, flanking towers, to allow the defenders to command—that is, to sweep with their crossbow fire—the lengths of wall between each pair of towers. More and more care was bestowed upon the defences of the entrance gateway, always the weak point in a castle or a walled town. The keep now tended to be relegated to the rearward or most inaccessible portion of the castle site, and to be regarded as a place of last resort, in which the garrison might hope to prolong their resistance if the rest of the castle had been stormed, either by rushing the gates or by scaling, mining, or breaching the curtain walls. This kind of castle is illustrated in a French example at Fig. 12.

A very important improvement was that the flanking towers now came to be built round instead of rectangular in outline. A round tower has two obvious advantages from the standpoint of defence. In the first place it has no angles. The angles are always the weak points, which an assailant will attack, either by trying to knock out the great corner-stones with a battering-ram, or by undermining the angle and so bringing down a good part of the

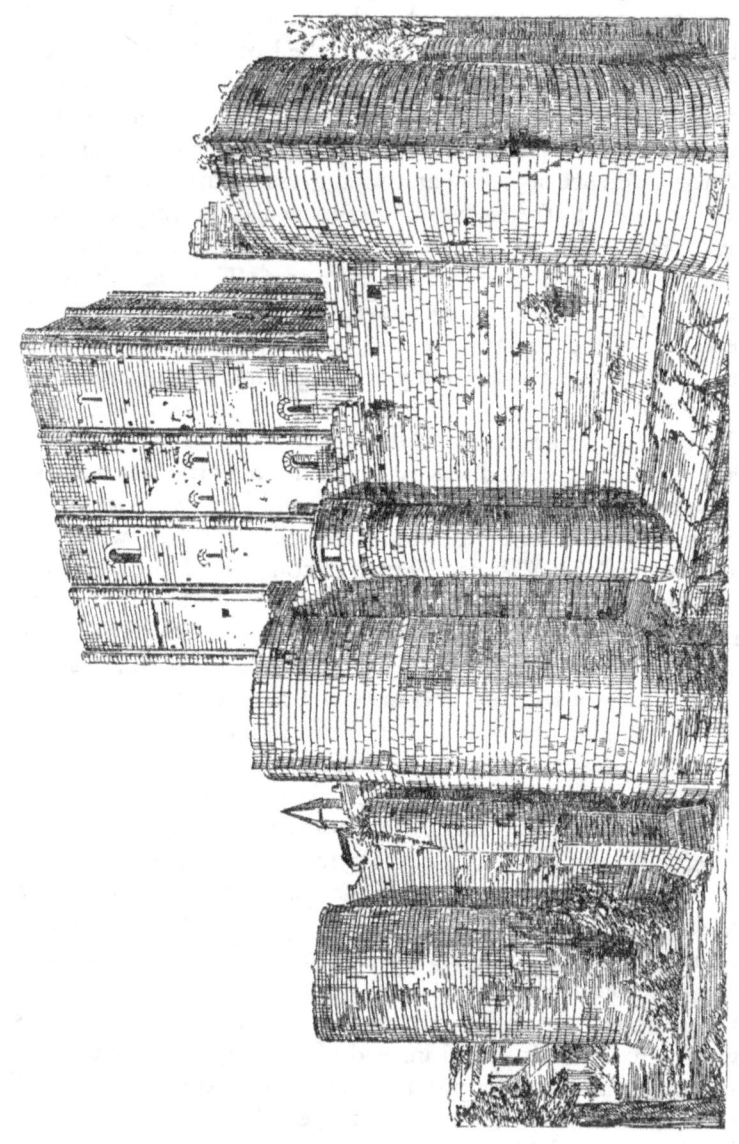

FIG. 12. The Château de Loches, a French castle showing Norman keep enclosed with a curtain wall and round towers in the thirteenth century.

COURTYARD CASTLES AND FORTIFIED MANOR-HOUSES

two adjoining walls. We have seen that this is what King John did at Rochester Castle in 1215. But a round tower had still another advantage over a square one. For it is clear that the corners of a square tower, besides being weak in themselves, are difficult to command by flanking fire from the curtain walls on either hand. Outside of each corner is a piece of 'dead ground', which it is hard for the archers to cover with their fire. No such difficulty exists in the case of a round tower. These advantages came to be fully realized by the western military engineers as a result of their experience in the Crusades.

At Framlingham Castle in Essex, built about 1200, we can see (Plate 3) the new importance of the curtain, which encloses a large area, with a wide and imposing sweep, and is protected by a whole array of flanking towers, like beads strung upon a necklace: but the towers are still of the old-fashioned rectangular pattern. On the other hand, Pevensey Castle in Sussex, built about thirty years later by Henry III, within the walls of an old Roman fort, shows the new round towers in all their pride (Fig. 13). The towers of the Roman fort are round too, and so at Pevensey we are reminded that it was from Roman or Byzantine fortifications in the Near East that the designers got the idea of making their flanking towers round.

In the outer walls of Kenilworth Castle, which were erected by King John, both round and square towers are found. Upon Kenilworth King John spent no less than £2,000—an enormous sum for that period. This castle is remarkable for the extent and elaboration of its water defences, though the lakes and moats by which it was once surrounded have long since been drained.

Of course the new idea was applied also to the keeps. So in the twelfth century, and in the earlier part of the thirteenth century, we find that a number of castles were built in which the keep is no longer square, but round. In addition to other advantages, such a round tower could be very easily covered over, on each floor, with a stone vault, rising to an apex like a dome: and in this way the keep could be made fireproof. One of the earliest and finest of these great round keeps is at Conisborough Castle in Yorkshire (Fig. 14). This has five large buttresses applied to the outside of the walls, in the fashion of the older square keeps. These buttresses are so large that one of them contains a very beautiful

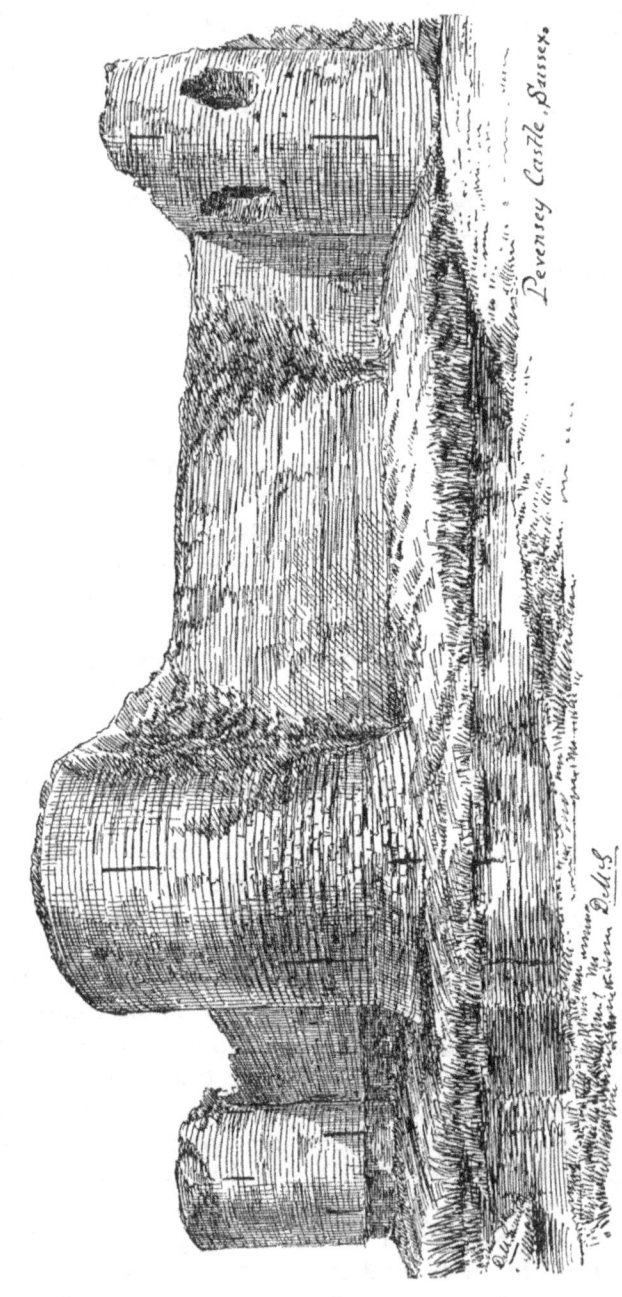

Fig. 13. Pevensey Castle: curtain walls and towers of the thirteenth century.

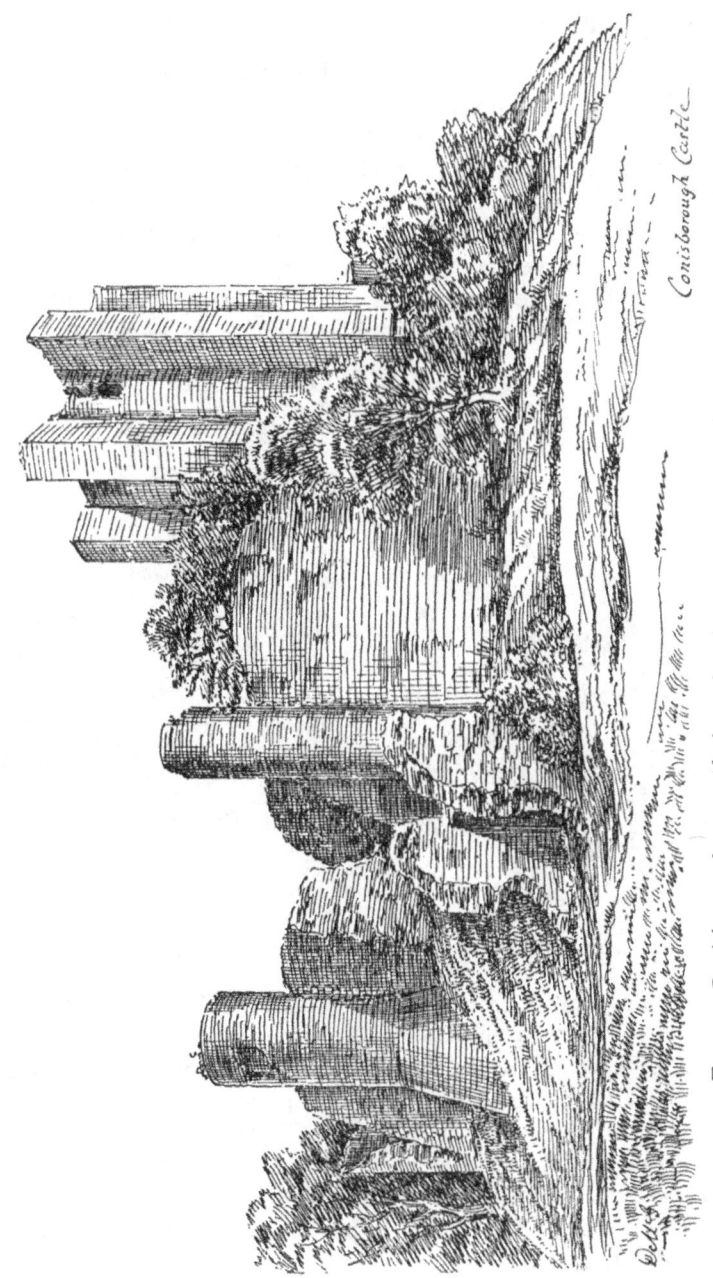

FIG. 14. Conisborough: general view, showing keep, curtain wall and round towers.

little chapel. Conisborough comes into *Ivanhoe*, and Scott thought it was a Saxon building, but it is in fact a Norman keep from the latter part of the twelfth century.

There is another great round keep, this time without buttresses, at Pembroke Castle in South Wales. Stimulated by the Crusades, the castle-builders of the West were now in the mood for experiments. So we have the remarkable keep at Orford in Suffolk, built by Henry II between 1165 and 1173. This is of multangular outline, and has three large rectangular projections, each big enough

FIG. 15. Bothwell Castle: a Scottish round keep (see p. 24).

to contain rooms. Even more unusual is Clifford's Tower, built after 1245 on the summit of William the Conqueror's *motte* in the Castle of York. Here the tower is in the form of a quatrefoil, like a four-leafed clover, and the interior rooms are planned very ingeniously. Here also, as at Duffus Castle, we can see what was apt to happen when a heavy stone tower was built upon an artificial mound. The walls of fine masonry have split and tilted forward, and in modern times they have had to be underpinned by a kind of concrete raft.

Comparatively few of these cylindrical keeps exist in Britain:

3. Framlingham Castle, from North-West

(See p. 45)

4. Harlech Castle. General view from the South, with Snowdon behind
(See pp. 59-62)

COURTYARD CASTLES AND FORTIFIED MANOR-HOUSES

for in the castle scheme the idea of the keep was by this time falling into disuse. The increased importance now given to the curtain wall, with its array of well-placed flanking towers, and the active defence which could be conducted upon this outer line, rendered the keep, with its powers of resistance that were mainly passive, obsolete. If the curtain wall with its towers were stormed, and the castle courtyard won, it was often difficult for the garrison amid the tumult to escape into the keep. If they did, their refuge might turn out merely to be a death-trap. Over in Normandy, Richard Coeur de Lion built, in 1197-8, his great Château Gaillard which was regarded as the most perfect piece of scientific fortification in its time. Here were both an outer and an inner curtain wall, both elaborately defended, and in front of the outer curtain, barring the only approach from which the castle on its rocky site could be attacked, was a great forework or barbican. Thus three successive lines of defence had to be overcome before the assailants were in a position to attack the mighty keep which dominates the whole. Now in 1204 Château Gaillard was captured by the French King after one of the greatest castle sieges in history. The assailants successively mastered the three enclosures mentioned above; but when the inner curtain was stormed the garrison at once surrendered, making no attempt to prolong their resistance in the keep. This clearly shows how the idea of the keep, as a last resort, was falling out of fashion.

Before taking leave of the Norman keeps, it is worth noting that the word is no older than the sixteenth century. The builders of a keep called it simply the great tower, or the *donjon*. This is the same word which has survived in modern speech as dungeon, meaning the prison of the castle, in which the feudal lord confined those sentenced in his baronial courts. Such a prison was usually placed in the basement of the keep. To be confined in a donjon therefore meant to be sent to prison, and so the word dungeon, which once signified the lord's great tower as a whole, has survived in its modern meaning of the prison which was provided in the lower part of many Norman donjons.

With the discarding of the keep as a place for final resistance, the idea grew up of treating each separate tower on the curtain wall as a single, self-contained defensive unit. So the doors leading

COURTYARD CASTLES AND FORTIFIED MANOR-HOUSES

into each tower from the courtyard were strongly secured by portcullises and iron-plated doors with drawbars: and similar obstacles were placed at the doors which led out from the towers to the wall-walks. Thus even if the besiegers had succeeded in breaking into the courtyard, each separate tower round the walls had to be seized before the castle was won. Soon, however, it became evident that the multiplication of such protective devices was a hindrance to the defenders themselves. It prevented them from moving freely round their castle to reinforce any part specially threatened. Moreover, it became hard to recapture a tower once taken. So in the later thirteenth century we find a growing wish to simplify the castle plan. Hand in hand with this went a tendency to reduce the size of the fortified enclosure. The attack and defence of fortifications was now a highly scientific business, and it was better to have a castle of manageable size, defended by a small garrison of picked and trained men, than one which needed a mob of untrained feudal levies.

In this way originated such a castle as Barnwell in Northamptonshire, built about 1266. The enclosure is comparatively small, and is rectangular in plan, with a round tower at three corners, while at the fourth stands the gatehouse, containing an entrance passage between two round towers. There is no donjon, and simplicity is the keynote of the whole design. In Scotland, Tibbers Castle in Dumfriesshire, built by an English knight in 1298, and the island castle of the Comyns at Lochindorb in Badenoch, are structures of this simplified, late thirteenth-century type.

Comparatively few castles of that period were erected in England. The baronage were by this time amply provided, and the strong Plantagenet kings frowned upon the building of more private strongholds. In the reign of Edward I there was thus a lull in castle building. It is in Wales, the country newly conquered by that king, that we find 'the magnificent badges of our servitude' as a Welsh writer[1] has described them—some of the noblest castles in the world.

It should be remembered that these great castles, with their high stone walls, flanking towers, and donjons, were the strongholds of kings and the powerful barons. The ordinary squire or landholder could not afford such structures. His defensive needs

[1] Thomas Pennant.

COURTYARD CASTLES AND FORTIFIED MANOR-HOUSES

were met by enclosing his residence with a moat, strengthened by a palisade. By the thirteenth century it was becoming common to build the hall and its appendages in stone. Many such moated stone manor-houses still survive in England. Yet the vast majority of the dwellings of the lesser gentry continued to be built of wood. These have long since perished, but the surrounding moats—'homestead moats', as they are called—are still to be found in almost every English parish. They are also present, though much less frequently, in Scotland.

In the great castles, too, we find the same arrangement of a dwelling-house consisting of a central hall, with the kitchen, pantry and buttery at its lower end, and the lord's private room at the upper. The buttery, of course, had nothing to do with butter, but was the place where the ale or wine was kept. The name is derived from an old French word *boterie*, represented in modern French by *bouteillerie*—the place for keeping bottles. In the great castles the hall with its appendages was, as a rule, massively built in stone. Often it was placed on the side of the castle courtyard furthest removed from the entrance, and was sometimes provided with a postern gate as a private means of escape. Harlech in Merionethshire and Kildrummy in Aberdeenshire provide examples.

At Aydon Hall in Northumberland there is still, in perfect preservation, a stone hall-house of the thirteenth century, arranged in the way I have described. Early in the next century, during the War of Scottish Independence, when the place became liable to raids from across the Border, Aydon Hall was enclosed by a stone wall with flanking towers, and so became quite a strong little castle—though of course it was not able to withstand a regular siege with all mechanical contrivances.

In the castle of Ashby-de-la-Zouch, which plays so prominent a part in *Ivanhoe*, there is a very fine hall, having the kitchen, buttery and pantry at its lower end, and the lord's private apartments at the upper. Behind the lord's rooms is a noble chapel, and all this beautifully illustrates the domestic accommodation deemed suitable for a powerful baron towards the end of the twelfth century. Although Sir Walter Scott says that the Ashby Castle of his story 'was not the same building of which the stately ruins now interest the traveller',[1] the hall at least is certainly as old as the reign of

[1] *Ivanhoe*, Chap. XIV.

Richard Coeur de Lion, and could well have been the scene of the banquet described by the novelist, in which Prince John was so rude to his Saxon guests.

In most of these castles the furniture was by this time quite ample, even by modern standards. In the body of the hall were massive oaken tables and long benches. The latter were laid on trestles, so they could be cleared away when the meal was over. On the dais the high table was like a modern one, and it could not be taken to pieces. Such a table was called a 'table dormant'. This high table might be richly carved, and the lord himself, his family and their distinguished guests would sit in high-backed, narrow chairs. Opposite to them, at the lower end of the hall, a band of minstrels played in a gallery above the screens; the latter now was often designed in a highly decorative manner. The walls of the hall were hung with fine tapestry, often imported from the Low Countries, and would be further decorated with stands of armour and trophies of the chase. Thomson in his *Autumn* wrote about

> 'ghostly halls of grey renown
> With woodland honours graced.'

The roof timbers of the hall would be curiously carved and painted. On its floor were strewn in summer rushes, and straw in winter: into this the relics of the feast were thrown, and household dogs quarrelled over the refuse. It was thought a proof of Archbishop Becket's extravagant living that in his hall the straw or rushes were changed every day! Thus the hall of an ancient castle must have been a smelly place; and so indeed was the castle as a whole, for the means of sanitation did not come up to modern standards, nor were people, as a rule, clean in their personal habits. The hall fireplace—a cavernous affair in which logs or peats were burnt—was often behind the hall table, so that the lord and his family should get the best of the heat. In larger castle halls there were sometimes two fireplaces, but many halls even at a much later period retained the primitive arrangement of a central open hearth, from which the smoke eddied uncomfortably through the hall, finally to escape—more or less—by means of an open lantern, or *louvre*, in the roof. By this time painted glass was becoming common in the greater castles. The lower parts of the windows were usually fitted with shutters, for the sake of ventilation.

COURTYARD CASTLES AND FORTIFIED MANOR-HOUSES

On the high table, the lord's dishes would by now be quite elaborate and curious affairs of green-glazed pottery, pewter, and silver, often gilt. The bedrooms of honour would contain massive carved bedsteads, with feather-beds, quilts, and elaborately decorated silken coverlets. The bed of a king or a great nobleman could be quite a grand affair. Thus Edward II's bed in Caerphilly Castle in 1326 had a canopy and curtains of red silk: the counterpane was of red silk lined with green silk, and there were two sheets, four pillows, and a coverlet of panelled silk lined with fur. The pillow coverlets were of wool, lined with fur. In those days people went to bed without any nightdress; and, as everybody was sorely afraid of nightly visits from ghosts or evil spirits, it was customary to have a night light by the bedside. As for the lesser folk and servants, these slept in bunks or on straw pallets, or even huddled together on the unsavoury floor of the hall.

There is no doubt that if one were compelled now to live in an ancient castle it would seem, for all its rude magnificence, cold, draughty, smelly, verminous, and thoroughly uncomfortable. But the folk of those days knew nothing better, and probably all of them, from the charcoal-burner in his woodland cabin to the baron in his lordly castle, were reasonably satisfied with their dwellings. Moreover, want of comfort indoors was probably less thought about than nowadays, for in ancient times men spent most of the daylight out of doors, and went to bed soon after dark.

In the Middle Ages there was no single person whose duties corresponded exactly to those of the modern architect. Instead, the lord of the manor placed the business in the hands of an official called the master of work. Now the master of work was not usually an architect, nor did he necessarily have any special acquaintance with the art of building. He was a man of business, trained in the conduct of affairs. In the earliest days, when education and administrative skill were largely confined to the Church, the master of work was often a clergyman. The word clerk, which today we use chiefly to describe a man skilled in conducting correspondence and office work, is the same in origin as the word clergyman; we refer still to a 'clerk in holy orders'.

The master of work would then engage a master mason, who

was responsible for the design and erection of the stonework of the castle. Of course he would have to suit his design to the wishes and ideas of the lord. Thus the master mason came nearest, in the building of ancient castles and churches, to the position of the modern architect. With the master mason, the master carpenter, master slater or tiler, master plasterer, and the other skilled craftsmen would work in conjunction; but all these were engaged directly by the master of work, who also bought the materials—stones or bricks, timber, slates or tiles, and so forth—which were required by each master craftsman. The master of work likewise paid all the bills and kept the accounts.

In the later Middle Ages, when education and business skill were no longer confined to the clergy, it sometimes happened that the master mason also acted as master of work, and then we have something very nearly approaching to the modern architect. For example, Master James of St. George, the master mason who designed Edward I's castles in North Wales, also acted as master of work. He was one of the great architects of the Middle Ages. He came from Savoy, which then belonged to the English Crown. But in general it is to the master mason, rather than the master of work, that we should ascribe the actual design of our ancient castles and churches. The names of many of them are known: as Henry of Reynes, for instance, architect of Westminster Abbey and of Clifford's Tower at York; Henry Yevele, who completed Westminster Abbey and was also a notable castle-builder; John Lewyn, who worked in northern England and was the architect of Bolton Castle in Wensleydale.

By the end of the thirteenth century England was well provided with castles. On the whole the policy of the kings was to discourage the building of new castles, at least on a large scale, for fear that the result might be to increase the power and independence of the greater barons. Thus it came about that in the English homeland few new castles of the first rank were founded during the reigns of Henry III and his son, Edward I. So the principal castle works of this period took the form of additions to existing castles, rather than the founding of new ones. Of course the greatest builders were the kings themselves. It is to this period that much of the outer walls and towers of the Tower of London

COURTYARD CASTLES AND FORTIFIED MANOR-HOUSES

and of Windsor Castle belong, as well as those of another great royal stronghold, Corfe in Dorsetshire. Henry III, the builder of Westminster Abbey, was a magnificent patron of fine architecture, and during his reign some notable additions were made to the internal accommodation of the royal castles. At Winchester he erected a splendid hall, which still exists, and his domestic buildings at Corfe, though now much ruined, have been of great beauty.

Perhaps the best example of a private or baronial castle which reached its final form during this period is Ludlow in Shropshire. Here is a Norman inner bailey or enclosure, behind high and thick stone walls with square flanking towers of the older fashion. On this line of walling is the keep or great tower, in the basement of which is the main entrance to the courtyard. Thus in this early castle we have a kind of combination of the keep and the gatehouse, a device which becomes very characteristic of the new castles erected by Edward I to hold down his conquests in Wales, upon the border of which Ludlow is situated. Within the courtyard there still remains a very beautiful and interesting Norman chapel, the nave of which is circular in plan, like that of the Temple Church in London, or the Norman church at Orphir in the Orkney Islands. Such churches, of which about half a dozen survive in Britain, were modelled upon the Church of the Holy Sepulchre at Jerusalem. Within the inner bailey at Ludlow is also a stately group of domestic buildings—kitchen, hall, solar and lodgings dating mostly from the reign of Edward I or later. Then there is the mighty outer bailey, strongly walled and furnished with towers both round and square; and the whole castle is embodied in the defences of a well-planned Norman town. Much of the town wall still survives. It seems to have been built in the reign of Henry III. The parish church, dedicated to St. Lawrence, dates from the fifteenth century. Nowhere in England can one better study a medieval castle, with its dependent town. Three miles to the south are earthworks of the earliest castle in Britain—a Norman castle built before the Norman Conquest. This is Richard's Castle, erected in 1032 by Richard Fitzcrob, one of the Norman favourites of Edward the Confessor. Like Cobbie Row's Castle in Wyre, it keeps its founder's name; and hard by it, as in Wyre, is the ancient parish church.

VII
The Edwardian Castles

In Wales, Edward I to secure his hold on the conquered land built some of the most magnificent castles to be seen anywhere. In Scotland there were no such castles; and it seems probable that one reason why there are none is that money to build them was lacking in the closing years of Edward's reign. But in this matter we must be cautious; for it is known that the Scots, when they dislodged the English, destroyed the castles in which the invaders had planted their garrisons; whereas, the Welsh not being so fortunate as to expel their oppressors, the castles remain to this day as monuments of the Plantagenet conquest. We know that Edward did carry out some building undertakings in Scotland, and some of his works indeed remain. Thus at Kildrummy Castle in Aberdeenshire there survives the stump of a great gatehouse that is undoubtedly his work, and we know that he planned to build another such structure at Linlithgow. The remains of a third gatehouse of the same kind, embodied in a later tower-house, have been identified at Dundonald Castle in Ayshire. Moreover, the great master masons who built the Welsh castles were also employed in Scotland. And at Tibbers Castle, Dumfriesshire, are the remains of a castle known to have been built in 1298 by an English knight in Edward's service. But there was probably nothing in Scotland to compare with the great castles of Wales.

These Welsh castles were like the national fortifications of the old Roman Empire or of modern states. They were public undertakings, built for public purposes and paid for out of public

THE EDWARDIAN CASTLES

money. The cost of building them was therefore entered in the public records, and so in the Exchequer Rolls we can follow the whole progress of their construction and add up exactly their total cost. For example, Harlech Castle in Merionethshire, perhaps the grandest of them all, was begun on 27 May 1285, and finished on 27 December 1291, at a total cost of £8,598 6s. 9d. As we should expect in the case of national defence works, these castles were planted on sites which commanded the conquered country. Not only this, but, in most cases, walled towns, carefully planned and laid out, and colonized by English settlers, were attached to the new castles. The King counted on his soldier burgesses to help him in maintaining law, and to spread settled life among the wild Welsh.

Of these North Welsh castellated towns by far the finest is Conway. The splendid town walls, with their three double-towered gateways and their one and twenty other round towers, remain almost perfect. Within, the town preserves its regular plan with a network of intersecting streets; and the fine town church retains some portions of an ancient monastery which stood on the site, but was transferred elsewhere by the masterful king when he laid out his new town. Over all, on its mighty rock, is the castle, likewise almost intact, with its outer and inner wards and its eight splendid round towers.

At Caernarvon, the most stately of all the castles, the regular plan of the town also survives, together with much of the walls. At Flint, the regular town plan again survives, but here the defences were of palisaded earthwork, and their banks and ditches may still be traced. In England, Edward I was the founder of Hull and Winchelsea, and at both the regular chess-board pattern of his town plan still remains. He was one of the great English town planners. There is no doubt that he got the idea of these new towns with their regular plans from Aquitaine, the dukedom which he held in southern France. Here such new towns—*villes neuves* or *bastides* as they were called—were a familiar feature, and Edward himself was the founder of more than one. In the south of France there were many Roman cities still surviving, and the idea of a regular town plan with a central market-place and an intersecting grid of streets had never been forgotten. The Romans laid out their marching camps and built their forts in the same way.

THE EDWARDIAN CASTLES

The first of the castles which Edward I built in North Wales was Flint (Fig. 16). Work there was started in 1277. It is clear from the plan that the design of the castle followed what may be called old-fashioned lines. It consists of a simple rectangular walled enclosure, with towers at all four corners, one of which is

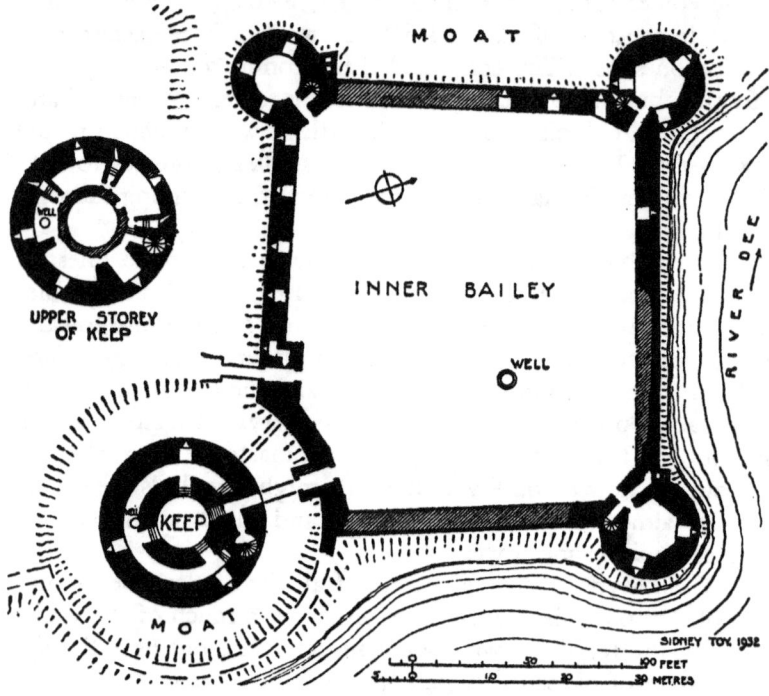

FIG. 16. Flint Castle: general plan.

extra large and forms the keep or donjon. It is isolated from the rest of the castle by its own ditch. We have seen that this kind of castle had been going out of use in England at least since the middle of the thirteenth century, and indeed Flint is the only one of Edward's castles to have this feature of a donjon. But instead of being kept in the rear as was usual in the older castles, at Flint the donjon was brought forward to the front of the castle. It immediately adjoins, and so protects, the entrance. This frontal massing of the weight of the castle shows a new idea, which became characteristic of the later castles built by Edward I in Wales. Moreover, the design of

THE EDWARDIAN CASTLES

the interior of the keep is most ingenious. On the ground floor the wall is enormously thick, and is traversed by a gallery running all round the tower, with three doors opening into the room in the interior. So if the entrance to the tower were forced, and the assailants succeeded in getting inside, the defenders could escape into the gallery, and moving round it, could sally forth by any one of the three doors against the assailants cooped up in the interior. The plan of Flint Castle, with its isolated donjon tower having a gallery running round inside its walls, is very like the plan of the castle and walled town of Aigues Mortes, in Provence. Aigues Mortes was a *bastide* or *ville neuve* founded by the crusading king, Louis IX—St. Louis—in 1244. Here Edward I, on his own crusade, spent some time in the summer of 1270; and it was from this port that he sailed for the Near East. There can be no doubt that Edward saw and admired the great donjon of Aigues Mortes and that he caused it to be imitated in the first castle that he built to hold down conquered Wales.

Flint may be copied from France, but to understand the ideas of Edward I and his architect, James of St. George, about the best design for a castle, we should go to Harlech in Merionethshire. This is the most grandly placed of all the Welsh castles. It is illustrated in Plate 4 and Fig. 17. From its battlements there is a magnificent view of the Snowdon range, and round its towers there clings a stern pathos that belongs alone to Harlech as the Castle of Lost Causes. It saw the glories of Owen Glendower's court in the last struggle for Welsh independence, and made the most desperate and protracted resistance to his English conquerors. Equally heroic was the long defence that it offered against Yorkist power in the cause of the Red Rose. And it was the last strength in Britain to haul down the royal standard of Charles I.

The castle stands upon the south end of its rock, and the craggy shelving slopes to the north have been walled in. This enclosure, however, is no part of the castle proper: the wall is mostly thin and low, and its chief purpose is to prevent unauthorized persons getting on to the rock, and so obtaining access to the sea-gate and the 'way from the marsh'. We know in fact that this outer wall was not added to the castle until 1295. We shall therefore consider only the main castle at the south end of the rock.

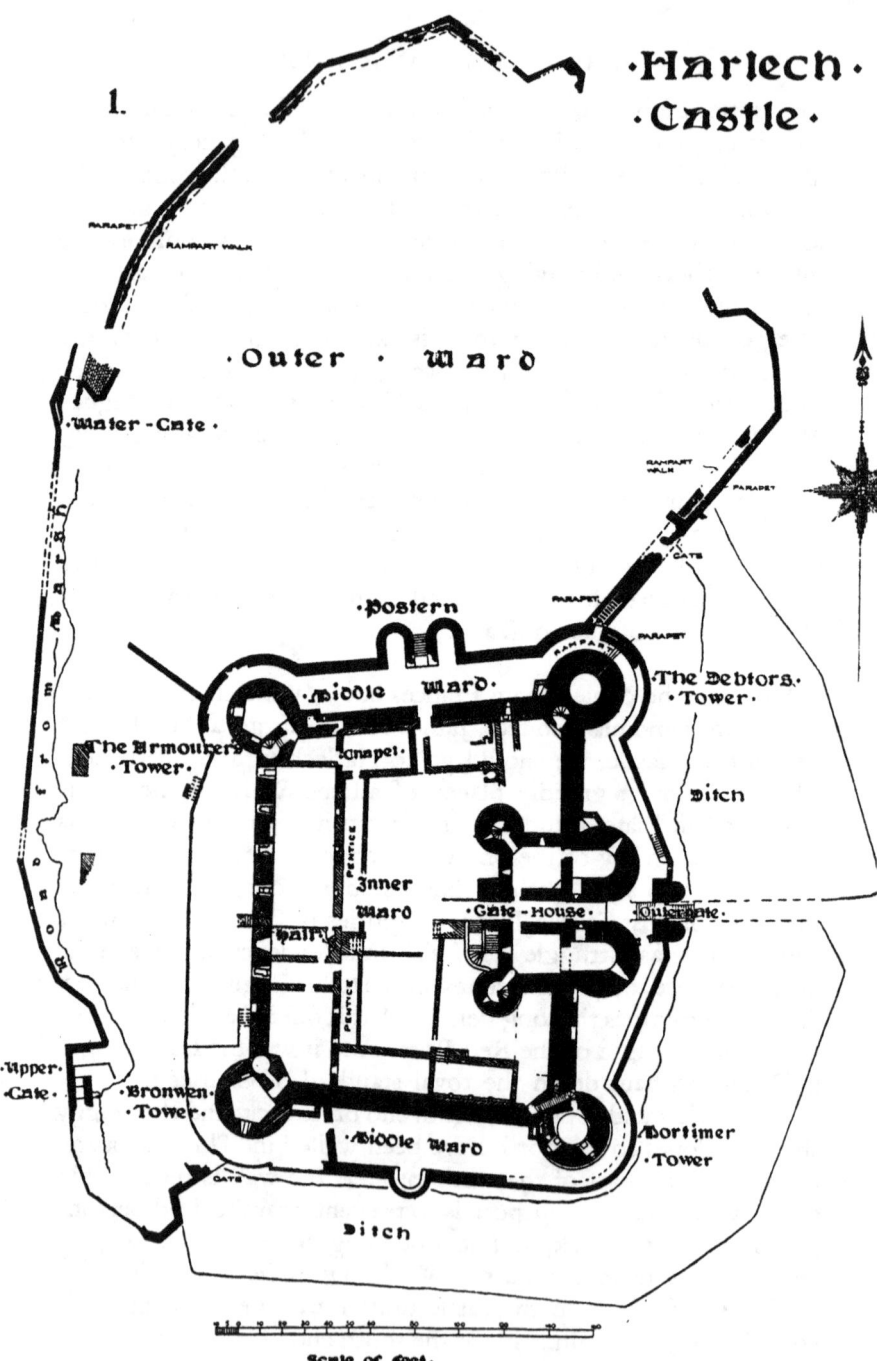

FIG. 17. Harlech Castle: general plan.

THE EDWARDIAN CASTLES

The first striking point is its symmetry. The castle consists of two enclosures, one wholly inside the other. I mentioned that at Château Gaillard there are no less than three such wards, but these are ranged one behind the other on the long narrow site; so they could only come into action *successively* against the attackers, as at the siege of 1204. Now at Harlech the outer ward *envelops* the inner one; and as its walls are low, while those of the inner ward are lofty, the defenders of the latter could shoot over the heads of the outer ward. So both wards could be in action simultaneously, instead of successively. This must have been a great advantage to the defenders.

A castle designed in this way may be called concentric; and these 'concentric' castles are in fact typical of the reign of Edward I. Neither he nor James of St. George invented the idea, for the Tower of London had been converted into a concentric castle in the reign of his father Henry III.

But this is not the only unusual feature at Harlech. There is no donjon or keep—neither in the old rearward position, as at Conisborough, nor brought forward to the front line, like the donjon of Flint; but instead, there is an enormous gatehouse—a lofty, oblong mass with the portal between two stout round towers in front, while at the two rearward corners, inside the courtyard, are smaller round towers, each housing a spiral stair. This gatehouse contains the entrance passage, defended by two—at first there were meant to be three—portcullises, by three pairs of folding gates, and by murder holes in the ceiling of the passage. Above all this, the upper floors of the gatehouse contain a complete set of living-rooms—hall, solar, chambers, and chapel, for the governor or constable of the castle, his family, and his personal staff. All this is quite separate from a large hall and other apartments provided on the other side of the courtyard for the general household or garrison of the castle.

So the lord of the castle, instead of securing himself in the safest position, instead of putting his trust in the purely passive defence of a keep or donjon situated at the remotest corner of the castle, now comes forward to an 'action front' position, facing the quarter from which attack was most to be dreaded, and having the whole defensive tackle of the entrance gateway—always the weakest point of any fortalice—under his immediate personal control.

THE EDWARDIAN CASTLES

At Flint, the keep had been brought forward to adjoin and cover the gatehouse; at Harlech the keep and the gatehouse have become one structure, which may be called a keep-gatehouse. And the keep-gatehouse, like the concentric plan, is characteristic of the Edwardian type of castle.

By now it is clear how much more confident and aggressive is the theory of defence that underlies the conception of the Edwardian castle. The older type of castle, like Château Gaillard, with its successive wards coming into action only one at a time, its donjon tucked away as a last resort in the most inaccessible quarter of the castle, was based on the theory that in the long run the attack is superior to the defence, that the successive wards will be captured one by one, until the critical moment comes when the garrison must seek to escape, if they can, into the last shelter of the donjon, there to make a final stand or await the slow agony of starvation. At Château Gaillard in the end, as we have seen, the donjon was not defended at all. In other words, the idea underlying the plan of the older castles was defeatism. Far other is the spirit of aggressive defence apparent in the concentric walls and frowning keep-gatehouse of an Edwardian castle.

King Edward's experiences during his Welsh campaign convinced him that a sea-link was vital to the security of a castle situated like Harlech. So in 1295, after the rising of Madoc-ap-Llewelyn, he caused the whole of the castle rock to be enclosed, and the remarkable sea-gate to be constructed, with its long and well-secured passage winding down to the Morfa Harlech.

At Rhuddlan in Denbighshire, and at Aberystwyth in Cardiganshire, are two more Edwardian castles. Both were begun in 1277 —the same year as Flint. Rhuddlan is still a stately and an interesting ruin, but of Aberystwyth unfortunately only fragments now remain. In each, the inner ward is lozenge-shaped, and there are two gatehouses, at opposite corners. But this plan with two gatehouses is best seen at the remarkable castle of Beaumaris (Fig. 18), in Anglesey. This was the last of Edward's castles to be begun. It was not founded until 1295, and the work of building it went on throughout his son's unhappy reign. The plan explains itself, and one notices its perfect geometrical symmetry. With a compass at the centre, one can draw a series of circles, each linking up the different towers and angles in their several positions, like a diagram of the sun with all its planets in their orbits. Beaumaris is as fine a castle to look at as its plan is beautiful to study; and again, this noble ruin commands a wonderful view of the Snowdon range, seen across the dancing waters of the Menai Strait.

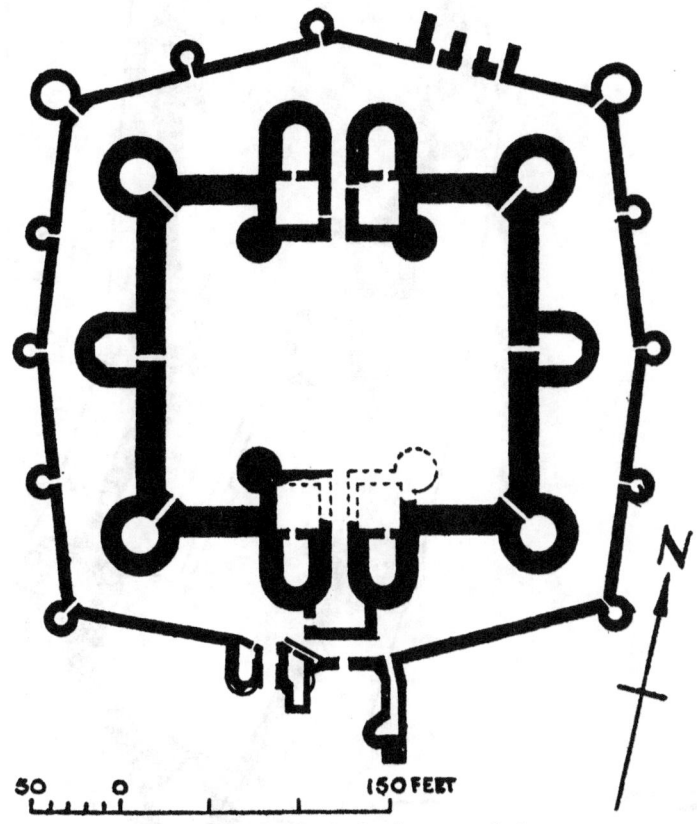

FIG. 18. Beaumaris Castle: general plan.

No doubt the most magnificent of the Edwardian castles in North Wales are Conway and Caernarvon. Yet neither of these is a concentric castle; for the long narrow sites did not allow of such a plan, and at Caernarvon, moreover (Fig. 19), things were complicated by the presence of a Norman *motte*, now removed. At both castles, therefore, we have a more or less oblong enclosure,

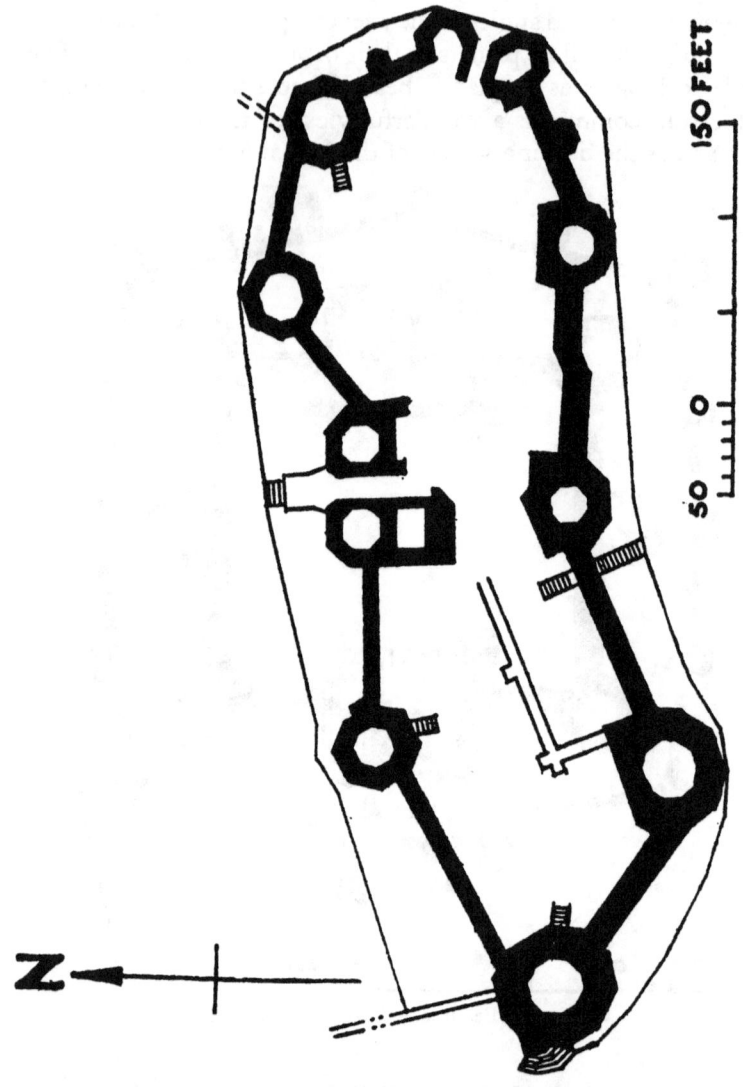

FIG. 19. Caernarvon Castle: general plan. The *motte* occupied the eastern enclosure. The Eagle Tower is at the west end. (See pp. 94-5.)

5. Caernarvon Castle, from the South
(See pp. 65, 94-5)

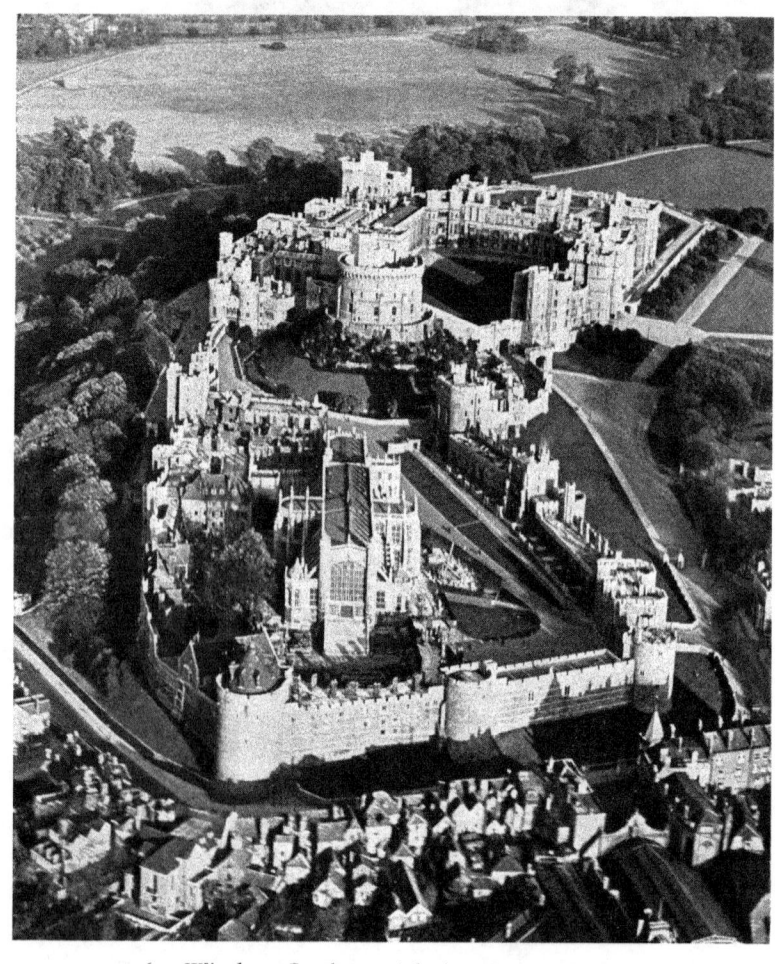

6. Windsor Castle: aerial view from the West
(See pp. 90-3)

divided by a cross wall into an inner and an outer ward—the whole being enclosed by a magnificent array of high walls and strong towers. At Conway the towers show the usual cylindrical outline, but at Caernarvon they are multangular, and it is this peculiarity, together with the banded masonry, which gives Caernarvon its distinctive aspect, as will be seen from Plate 5. These bands are made of a light-coloured limestone and a darker sandstone. But if Caernarvon Castle has no concentric arrangement of wards, it has two magnificent Edwardian gatehouses; though the larger, the King's Gate, was never finished. The entry through this formidable structure was defended by a drawbridge, five pairs of folding gates, and six portcullises—not to speak of a series of murder holes in the vaulted ceiling of the passage, and bow-slits opening in the side walls! Rather curiously, Caernarvon retains the old-fashioned feature of a donjon, the famous Eagle Tower, which obviously was designed as a dwelling for the King, or for the Prince of Wales when in residence.

This splendid castle shows very clearly the new idea of defence by a small garrison of picked men, able to move freely all round the building, instead of the older idea in which each tower was isolated and considered as a separate post. On the seaward front of the castle, which was the first part to be built and shows the full original design, there are two tiers of passages running the whole length of the walls, so as to connect tower with tower. These galleries are well furnished with bow-slits; and over all was the open wall-walk. There was thus a triple-tiered line of defence. Many of the bow-slits are arranged in groups of three, converging upon one external loophole, so that three archers, shooting by turns, could serve each loophole. On the battlements the archers were protected by swinging wooden shutters hung in the embrasures.

In magnificence and beauty, Caernarvon Castle stands out among all the Edwardian strongholds in North Wales. The others are, upon the whole, sturdy business-like affairs; but Caernarvon was obviously designed not only as a great fortress, but as the seat of the royal government and a palace for the Prince of Wales. Visiting it in the time of Cromwell, an English traveller has recorded his impression of the castle and town in language which nobody could better. At Caernarvon, so he says:

THE EDWARDIAN CASTLES

'I thought to have seen a town and a castle, or a castle and a town: but I saw both to be one, and one to be both: for indeed a man can hardly divide them in judgment or apprehension: and I have seen many gallant fabrics and fortifications, but for compactness and completeness of Caernarvon I never yet saw a parallel. And it is by art and nature so fitted and seated that it stands impregnable; and if it be well manned, victualled and ammunitioned, it is invincible, except fraud or famine do assault, or conspire against it.'[1]

I have mentioned already that the concentric castle was not the invention of Edward I or James of St. George. Nor was the King the first or only builder of such castles. What in the end became the most elaborate of all concentric castles, and, in regard to the sheer area that it covered, perhaps the largest castle in Britain, was begun in 1271—while Henry III was still on the throne—by a great English nobleman, Gilbert de Clare, ninth Earl of Gloucester, and Earl of Hereford. This is Caerphilly Castle in Glamorgan, near Cardiff (Fig. 20). Earl Gilbert—the Red Earl, men called him—was married to a daughter of Edward I. He was one of the marcher barons, as they were styled; one of the English lords who had won themselves estates in the marches or borderlands between England and Wales. They lived in constant warfare with the Welsh, and so they had to house themselves in formidable castles, not less strong nor sometimes less magnificent than those which Edward I himself was building to hold down the same heroic people. Elsewhere in England, as we have seen, few large castles were being built; for the King frowned upon the erection of any more private strongholds in a realm already amply provided. So it comes about that the last of the really great castles erected in the realm of England were those founded in Wales by Edward I and the most powerful of his marcher barons. Earl Gilbert, as lord of Glamorgan, founded Caerphilly as a stronghold designed to protect his territories against the power of Llewelyn-ap-Gruffyd, the last native Prince of Wales. Here also, according to the same policy as was afterwards adopted by Edward I, a walled borough was planned in dependence on the castle.

---

[1] John Taylor, *A Short Relation of a Long Journey*, 1650—quoted in the *Official Guide* to Caernarvon Castle, p. 3.

THE EDWARDIAN CASTLES

Caerphilly Castle took a long time to build, and there is evidence that considerable alterations were made in the design while the work was going on. In its final form, and including the water defences, the whole thing covers an area of no less than thirty acres. The central part is a concentric castle, very like Harlech, with outer and inner wards, but having a double gatehouse like

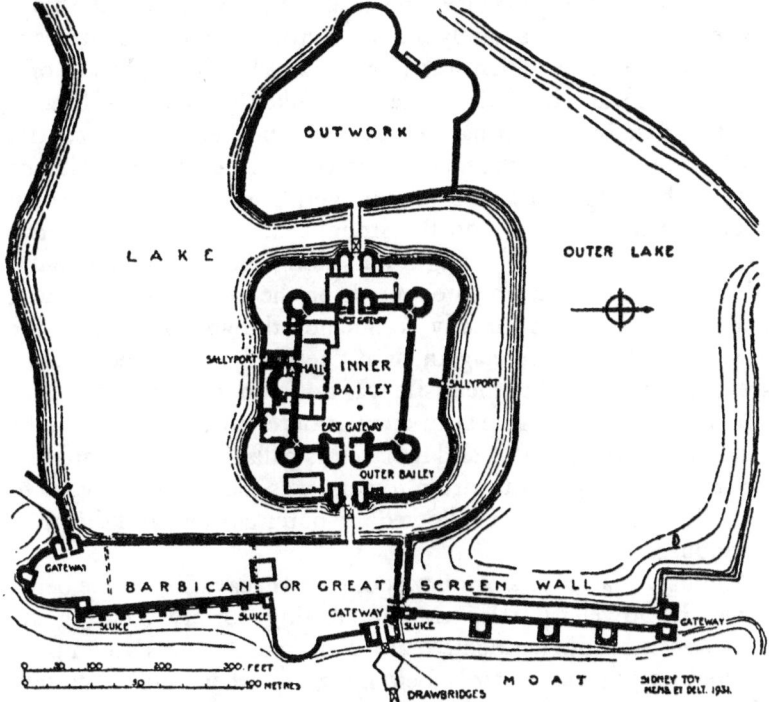

FIG. 20. Caerphilly Castle: general plan.

Beaumaris. In addition to this, there is a third large enclosure, quite separate from the main castle, on the western side; and on the eastern side a huge fortified barrage, about 400 yards in span, was thrown across the valley, damming the two streams so as to turn the whole site into a lake, about 12 feet deep, and large enough to enclose not only the main castle but the western outwork. This dam, with its massive buttresses to resist the pressure of the water, reminds one for all the world of the barrages or dams which the hydro-electric boards are today building in so many valleys.

Besides serving its purpose of retaining the waters of the lake, it most skilfully turned to account a part of the defences of the castle.

Caerphilly is certainly a masterpiece. It was blown up with gunpowder during Cromwell's wars, but a large part of it was very carefully restored by the late Marquis of Bute, and it gives now a splendid idea of an ancient castle as a going concern. One thing, however, the Marquis wisely did not restore: the celebrated Leaning Tower, half of which was blown away by the explosion of a mine, while the other half is tilted over like the Tower of Pisa.

At Kidwelly, in Carmarthenshire, is another fine concentric castle, built by one of the marcher barons. But as this castle stands with its back against a steep slope overhanging a river, the plan is like a half-moon; for on the straight side the two wards run together so as to form a single wall along the edge of the bank. Also here the great keep-gatehouse is on the outer line of defence, not on the inner. It directly commands the approach from the town of Kidwelly. Here again, as at Caerphilly, these peculiarities are due to the fact that the castle was not all built at one time, nor after a single design. The semi-circular outer curtain stands on the bank of a Norman castle, and replaces its palisade. The rectangular inner ward, with its four drum towers, was the first stonework to be built on the site; later followed the outer curtain, and the great gatehouse.

About a quarter of a century ago, when excavations were being made at Kidwelly Castle, some interesting pottery was dug up. This consisted of fragments making up more or less a complete pitcher or jug, and sherds belonging to other similar vessels. What marked these vessels out from the rest of the pottery found at the same time is the fact that they were decorated with leaf patterns in green and brown. Now similar pottery has been found at a number of sites in widely distant parts of Britain, but always at ports or places near the coast. London has yielded the largest number. It is believed that this kind of painted ware came from southern France, probably from Bordeaux, which in those days belonged to the English kings. There was a brisk trade in wine between Bordeaux and England, and it may have been in this way that these polychrome jugs, as they are called, reached Kidwelly.

VIII
More about Edwardian Castles

WE have seen how in South Wales a great marcher nobleman built himself a concentric castle larger and more elaborate than anything that his royal master was putting up in the Snowdon country. It is true that Caerphilly Castle was begun in the reign of the weak king, Henry III. Whether Gilbert de Clare bothered to obtain from his successor—perhaps the strongest of English monarchs—permission to continue his work at Caerphilly, we do not know. Possibly he didn't, for these marcher barons enjoyed much independence and many privileges to which they fiercely clung.

But in North Wales, while the King was founding his castles and their associated boroughs in the conquered land, another nobleman was building a new town and castle on his own, and on a scale fully equal to the royal undertakings. It is known that here both castle and borough were founded with the King's assent and as part of his programme for the pacification of Wales.

Henry de Lacy, Earl of Lincoln and Salisbury, was one of the most powerful barons of his time, and a favourite of Edward I. In the conquest of North Wales he had rendered his sovereign notable assistance. His reward, in 1282, was a grant of the lordship of Denbigh, in order that he might erect a castle there and hold the district down. Building was started immediately, and before the end of the year six royal masons were being employed on the job.

At Denbigh, as at Conway and Caernarvon, town and castle were planned together. As at Caernarvon, the castle stands in a corner of the town site, so that part of the town wall also forms part of the castle. This section of the wall, the earliest bit of the castle to be built, shows the usual round towers of the time, very like those of the town walls at Conway and Caernarvon. But when the builders took in hand the front of the castle towards the town, we find something utterly different: the curtains are thicker and better built, and there are large multangular towers with passages in the thickness of their walls, like those at Caernarvon. Moreover there is a marvellous gatehouse, consisting of three great octagonal towers, set at the points of a triangle, with an octagonal entrance hall between them and a crooked entrance passage, very strongly defended. Now at Caernarvon Castle there is evidence that the King's Gate, had it been completed, would have contained just such a crooked passage, with a central octagonal gate-hall.

So it cannot be doubted that when the front of Denbigh Castle facing the town came to be built, King Edward lent Earl Henry his architect, Master James of St. George. But the work was paid for by the Earl, since it does not appear in the public accounts. Thus Denbigh Castle, though built as the private stronghold of a feudal baron, was really founded as an instrument of national policy, part of the royal measures for the pacification of North Wales. It shows the old type of private castle, under the wise control of a powerful king, passing into the kind of public defence work that we find in a modern state.

I have described how at Caernarvon the multangular walls and towers are banded with different colours of stone. The great gatehouse of Denbigh Castle shows similar decorative treatment, only here it is done by blocks of dark and light stone arranged chequerwise. Also at Caernarvon and Denbigh there is a statue of the King over the main entrance.

Master James of St. George's liking for multangular towers, instead of the round ones then in fashion, is most intriguing. Before he came over to Britain, he had erected in his native country, for the Count of Savoy, a castle which also had multangular towers. This was St. George d'Esperance, near Lyons—the town from which James probably took his name. At the Château de Trevoux, also not far from Lyons, there is another great octagonal tower with banded masonry, and this is perhaps also the work of Master James. Quite likely the idea of octagonal towers with banded stonework was brought back from the Crusades; for the Roman walls and towers of Constantinople are built in this way, and they very closely resemble those at Caernarvon Castle.

Before leaving the castles planted by Edward I in North Wales, let us consider for a moment how great was his achievement. Flint, Rhuddlan, Conway, Caernarvon, Harlech, Beaumaris, Aberystwyth—and Builth in Breconshire, of which little save the earthworks remains. Then there were the castles built at the same time by private lords, but with the King's approval and support, and as part of his general scheme. I have mentioned Denbigh, but there were also Chirk and Ruthin, important Denbighshire castles. And there were the three native Welsh castles which Edward took over and refashioned to serve his own ends—Criccieth and Dolwyddelan, both in Caernarvonshire, and Castell-y-Bere in Merioneth.

We have to imagine the cost and the tremendous organization required to carry out this vast programme of castle building: the accumulation of men, materials and supplies in remote and inaccessible, indeed dangerous localities; the formidable problems of transport; the organization of the labour force; the protection of the working parties; the detailed and accurate accounting. To take one single instance only, at Beaumaris Castle in 1296 Master James of St. George was directing the operations of 400 masons, 2,000 labourers, 200 quarrymen, 30 smiths and carpenters, 100 carts, 60 wagons, and 30 cargo boats! Then there was all the legal and administrative business—the problem of land surveying alone—involved in founding the new boroughs and filling them with English colonists.

No such immense programme of systematic fortification had been seen in Britain for a thousand years—not since the Romans built their chain of forts along the Saxon shore. No such programme would be seen again until Henry VIII and Elizabeth I protected the shores of their realm with fortifications designed for defence by the new artillery.

Gilbert de Clare, the Red Earl of Gloucester, who founded Caerphilly Castle, also possessed an important castle at Tonbridge in Kent. To this castle either he, or perhaps his son, also Gilbert,

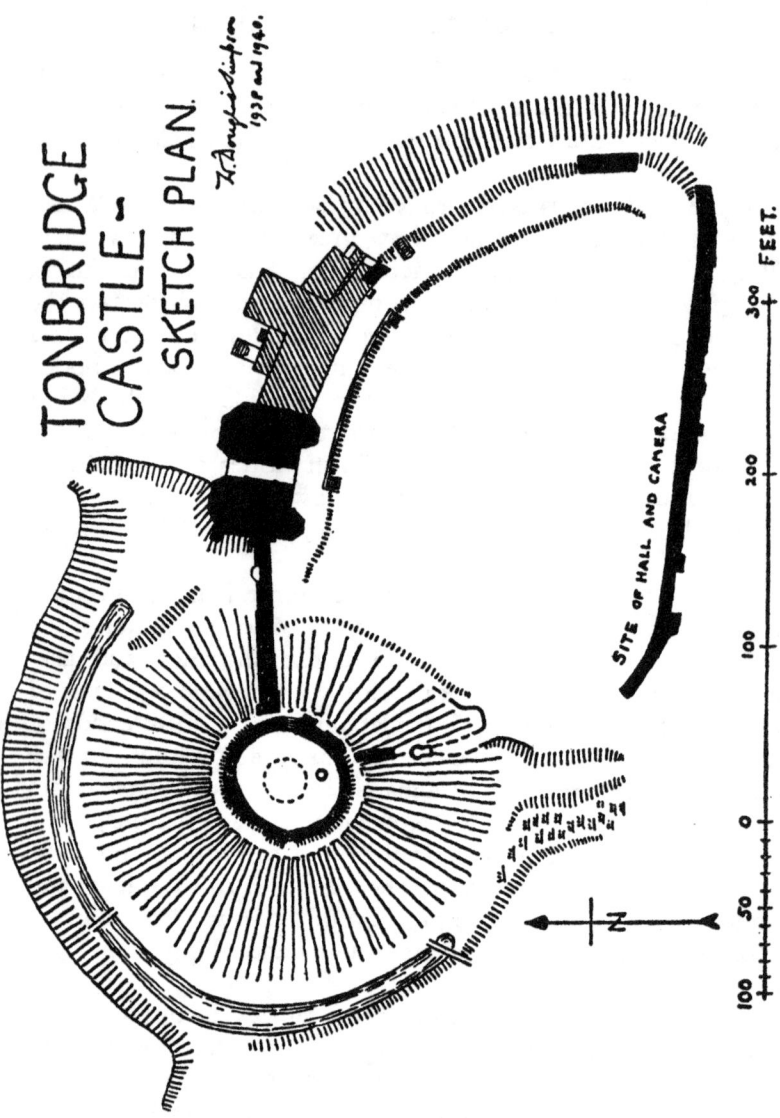

FIG. 21. Tonbridge Castle: general plan.

who succeeded in 1295 and fell at Bannockburn in 1314, added a keep-gatehouse. It closely resembles those of Caerphilly and Harlech, but is even more strongly defended. In fact, the defences of this Tonbridge gatehouse are more formidable than anything of the kind that I have seen in Britain.

Tonbridge Castle (Figs. 21, 22) is one of the most instructive in England. It was in existence by 1088, in which year it was captured by William Rufus. Like so many Norman castles, it began as a mount-and-bailey. The site is a good one, on the north bank of the Medway. The *motte*, large and lofty, is at the west end, and the bag-shaped bailey extends eastward downstream. To the north lies the town. The way in which the town ditches are worked into those of the castle makes me feel that castle and town were planned together, as at Ludlow and Appleby. All the ditches were wet, and some of them still hold water.

I think the first part of the castle to have its timber defences replaced by stone was the bailey. Part of the wing-wall that climbs up to the *motte* shows Norman masonry, with its characteristic square-faced stones. No doubt this was built in the twelfth century. Early in the next century—to judge by the stonework—a shell-keep was built on top of the *motte*. This was known later as the dungeon—that is, of course, the donjon tower. In 1531 it still had a lead roof; so probably it was designed as the lord's residence.

But later in the thirteenth century the lord of Tonbridge began to get tired of living in his cramped donjon on top of the *motte*. So down he came into his spacious bailey, and there he built himself a stately hall, with chambers attached, overlooking a pleasant reach of the Medway. This sort of thing happened often in that century, when the lords began to desert their gloomy keeps to provide convenient lodgings for themselves in the castle courtyard.

But this was not the end of developments at Tonbridge. The entrance to the bailey must always have been on the north side from the town. I don't know what sort of an affair the early gateway may have been, but about the year 1300 it was replaced by a keep-gatehouse of formidable size and strength, and of unusual magnificence and beauty in decoration. Clearly it was designed to provide strong and stately quarters for the lord of the castle when in residence, and for the castellan in the lord's absence.

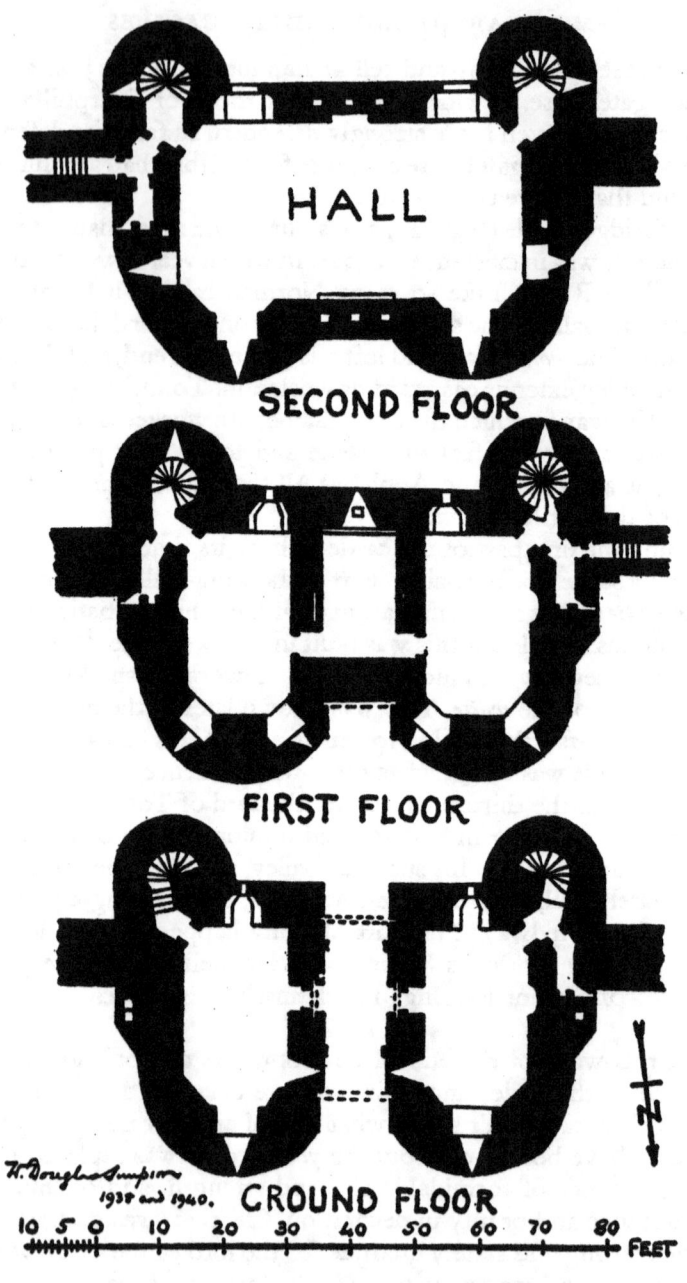

FIG. 22. Tonbridge Castle: plans of gatehouse.

MORE ABOUT EDWARDIAN CASTLES

Like those at Caerphilly, Harlech and Beaumaris, Tonbridge gatehouse (Fig. 22) forms an oblong mass, with two large round towers in front, on either side of the entrance, while on the inner side two smaller round towers contain the spiral staircases. The entrance was defended by a drawbridge, which when raised formed an extra barrier to the portal. Within, the passage was secured by front and rear portcullises, and by two pairs of folding gates. The inner pair closed against the courtyard—so that, by these and by the rear portcullis, the gatehouse could be defended against an enemy who had gained possession of the castle courtyard. In the vault of the entrance passage is a series of murder holes.

On either side of the passage, doors lead into the rooms in the two towers. One of these was the guard-room, the other a store. The extraordinary feature of this Tonbridge gatehouse is that even these inner doors are each provided with a portcullis. Thus still further obstacles were put in the way of an assailant who had mastered the entrance passage, before he could obtain access to the two stairs which lead to the upper floors of the gatehouse.

Below the towers on each side is an underground room. One of these was a cellar, the other the castle prison.

The first floor of the gatehouse formed a fighting-deck, manned by the crews who served the drawbridge, portcullises, murder holes and the bow-slits that swept the approaches. It was divided into three compartments. The central one was the portcullis room. Those on either side provided quarters for the garrison.

Above this, on the second floor, was the lord's hall. This has been one of the noblest rooms of its kind in England. It is beautifully fitted up, with a stately fireplace and spacious windows, all designed in the richest Gothic style. Here even a king might deem himself bravely housed.

Another room above this was evidently intended, and this would have contained the private apartments of the lord and his family. But it is doubtful if this storey was ever completed.

So careful were the designers of this keep-gatehouse to isolate it from the rest of the castle, that even the doorways out to the wall-walks on the curtains in either side were each provided with a stout door and portcullis. Small wonder that a royal official in 1521 could call this 'as strong a fortress as few be in England'.

MORE ABOUT EDWARDIAN CASTLES

So in the wild days of the Conquest the lord of Tonbridge took up his quarters, for security reasons, high on his earthen *motte*, dominating alike the bailey of his castle below and the town that huddled under the shelter of his ramparts. There in safety he sat, protected by his own ditch from the bailey should his enemies gain it—protected also by its steep, slippery sides and the stout oaken palisade (and later by the stone shell-wall) on top. Then in the thirteenth century, in this settled and kindly corner of England, he descended from his cramped, uncomfortable *motte* and sought more pleasant housing in a spacious new hall by the riverside. But about the turn of this century the lord moved once again. Forsaking his sunny hall, he crossed over his courtyard and housed himself afresh in a formidable gatehouse, fronting the direction from which attack was most to be feared, yet equally well secured against his own castle behind him.

What does the last move mean?

In particular, how shall we explain the building of so tremendous a fortification in the peaceful home county of Kent about the year 1300? To build such a keep-gatehouse in the wild Welsh borderland was quite another matter. On the throne then sat the strongest of English kings. We know that he did not like his subjects to build private castles in England, whatever he might have encouraged them to do among the wild Welsh or stubborn Scots. We may be certain that this keep-gatehouse at Tonbridge was not put up without Edward I's consent.

For many years the Earls of Gloucester, like other marcher barons, had pursued a policy hostile to the Crown. Not without good reason, they feared that the conquest of North Wales would lead to an attack upon their own privileges. Much of the Red Earl's life had thus been spent in bitter opposition to Henry III and Edward I. But in 1290 there came about a reconciliation. The Red Earl married the King's daughter, Joan of Acre. Thereafter both he, and his son while the old King lived, were, upon the whole, supporters of the Crown.

Now in 1295 came the crisis of King Edward's reign. Scotland and Wales were both blazing in revolt. On top of all this, the King found himself plunged into a great continental war. England, Holland, Flanders, Brabant, Savoy, Anjou, and the 'King of the Romans' all stood together against France. As usual, Edward was at his wits' end for money. Burdened with his wars in Wales and Scotland, he had neglected home defence. England had lost command of the narrow sea, and, to the King's wrath and shame, the French landed and gave Dover to the flames.

So Edward, and his barons who held castles between London and the coast, had to look to their defences. Since Tonbridge lies on the highroad from Hastings to London, we can surely understand the reason for the building of so formidable an addition to its fortifications just at this critical period.

We have seen that extraordinary care was taken to secure the keep-gatehouse, not only against an attack from outside, but also from inside the castle. Of course such precautions would have been valuable, supposing that an enemy had succeeded in gaining the castle courtyard from the rear, by breaching, mining, or scaling the walls. But this is not the whole reason.

I have said that it is a mistake to think of an old castle as always garrisoned by a picked body of men-at-arms, ready for instant action. On the contrary, in time of peace there would be few if any armed men within its walls. Should war approach, the lord or constable would defend his castle by calling up his vassals who dwelt around, and who were bound to render military service to their overlord.

Now this was all very well in the earlier days of warfare, but by the time of Edward I, warfare had become an extremely serious matter. Campaigns were now fought out with large, well-organized and well-trained forces; and they took a long time to decide. In particular, the attack and defence of fortified places had become an elaborate science. For such work the untrained feudal levies, fresh from the plough, were utterly unsuited. Moreover, they were, as a rule, not bound to do more than forty days' service in a year. And in some cases their liability to serve was restricted to the homeland, or to following the King in person. Thus when Edward I called up his feudal barons for the continental campaign of 1295, some of them flatly refused to go overseas. 'By God, Sir Earl,' swore the King to one of them, 'thou shalt either go or hang!' 'By that same oath, Sir King,' replied the Earl, 'I will neither go nor hang!'

Under these new conditions the monarchs of western Europe

in their wars, and the nobles in their private quarrels, everywhere began to exchange or commute the military service due them by their vassals for rents, payments in money or in kind. With the money so obtained the lord could hire professional soldiers, skilled men of war who would follow his banner anywhere and for so long as he had cash to pay them.

So all over western Europe, though the feudal levies were still called out on grand occasions, wars were coming to be fought more and more by means of paid professional soldiers. Thus in his Welsh and Scotch campaigns, both Edward I and his barons used these two kinds of troops—the feudal levies, and professional soldiers whom they hired, often from overseas.

Castles now had to find quarters for standing garrisons of mercenaries. But such troops were something very different from the short-term feudal levies, unwarlike country-folk turned into soldiers for the occasion. The mercenaries had none of the natural allegiance of a vassal to his overlord. At all times they were liable to turbulence or treachery—particularly if their employer's enemy was able to offer them higher wages. At the worst, they might be a source of danger to the lord in his castle; at the best, unruly neighbours. So everywhere in western Europe we find the lords tending to shut off themselves, their families, and their personal retainers, in a self-contained part of the castle, capable of being held against the paid garrison should the latter revolt, and having the entrance gateway, always the first objective of treachery, under their own control.

This is one of the reasons that led to the development of the keep-gatehouse as a feature of many large castles built round about the year 1300. In England, this development did not go much further, because castles of any kind were now gradually ceasing to be built. The comparative unity of the country, strength of the central government and absence of private warfare, were putting an end to the military side of feudalism. In France and Scotland, on the other hand, feudal anarchy and the tyranny of the barons reached their worst during the fourteenth and fifteenth centuries. So in these countries the new type of castle, designed for a standing garrison of mercenaries, became a very formidable affair indeed.

This attempt to combine, in one and the same building, a fortified gatehouse with the lord's private lodging, was bound to cause problems. In a medieval house it was usual to place the hall on the first floor, raised upon cellars; but in a keep-gatehouse the first floor was needed as a fighting-deck. It had to house the men to manage and the tackle to hoist the drawbridge and the portcullises, and to take up station at the murder holes. So the great hall has to be sent upstairs to the second floor, an awkward arrangement.

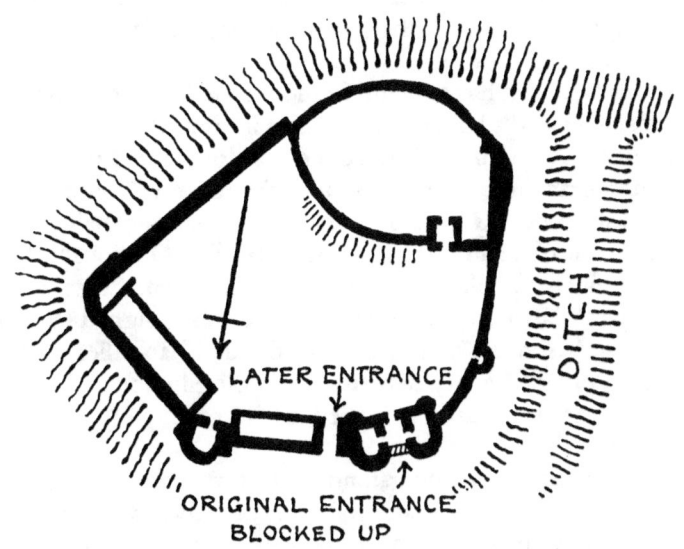

Fig. 23. Llanstephan: sketch plan.

West of Kidwelly in Wales, across the sandy estuary of the Towy, perched on a green hilltop is the noble castle of Llanstephan (Fig. 23). Upon the highest part of the enclosure is the inner ward, probably the oldest part of the castle, with a small square tower of entrance. In front of this is the much larger outer ward or main enclosure, well walled and towered, and having a keep-gatehouse reminiscent of Tonbridge. Here also the great hall is on the second floor, the first floor being given over as a fighting-deck from which the fore and rear portcullises and the murder holes were worked. Later owners found this so inconvenient that they walled up the entrance passage, converting it into a cellar, and opened up a new gateway into the curtain wall close beside. Thus the old keep-gatehouse was converted into a tower-house pure and simple. There could be no clearer proof of the practical awkwardness of trying to combine the gatehouse of a castle with the lord's residence.

But Llanstephan has something more to tell about the new kind of castle. The lord's hall, on the second floor of the gatehouse, has been a fine stateroom, with traceried windows and a rich fireplace —not unworthy to be compared with the room at Tonbridge. But in the eastern corner of the courtyard is a second hall, twice as large as the lord's hall but plain and barn-like. Obviously this has been the garrison hall—a barrack or mess room. Close beside it are the men's latrines. Llanstephan Castle was designed to house a standing garrison. As marcher lords, the de Chamvilles who built it were involved in every row that was going in South Wales, and the history of their castle is indeed a wild one.

It is impossible to understand castles without an eye on the shape of contemporary history. Much of Edward II's reign was filled with the uproar of a strife between the King and his overpowerful cousin, Thomas Plantagenet, Earl of Lancaster. This turbulent nobleman held no less than five Earldoms—Lancaster, Leicester, Derby, Lincoln and Salisbury. Unhappily his abilities and public spirit were unequal to the enormous power which these possessions gave. In Marlowe's *Edward II*, Piers Gaveston refers scornfully to Earl Thomas as:

> 'The mighty Prince of Lancaster
> That hath more Earldoms than an ass can bear.'[1]

Among his broad lands Earl Thomas held the barony of Embleton, on the wild Northumbrian coast not far south of Berwick-upon-Tweed. Here in 1313 he began to build himself one of the grandest of English castles. The proud Plantagenet prince did not wait to procure from his royal cousin a licence for the work,

---
[1] Marlowe, *Edward II*, Act I, Sc. iii.

7. Greenknowe Tower: view from South-East
(See p. 107)

8. Coxton Tower: view from South-West
(See pp. 111-14)

MORE ABOUT EDWARDIAN CASTLES

which was not granted him until three years later. To his new castle he gave the name of Dunstan's borough, from the neighbouring township of Dunstan.

Dunstanburgh Castle (Fig. 24) is the largest in Northumberland: the ruins cover no less than eleven acres. They are superbly

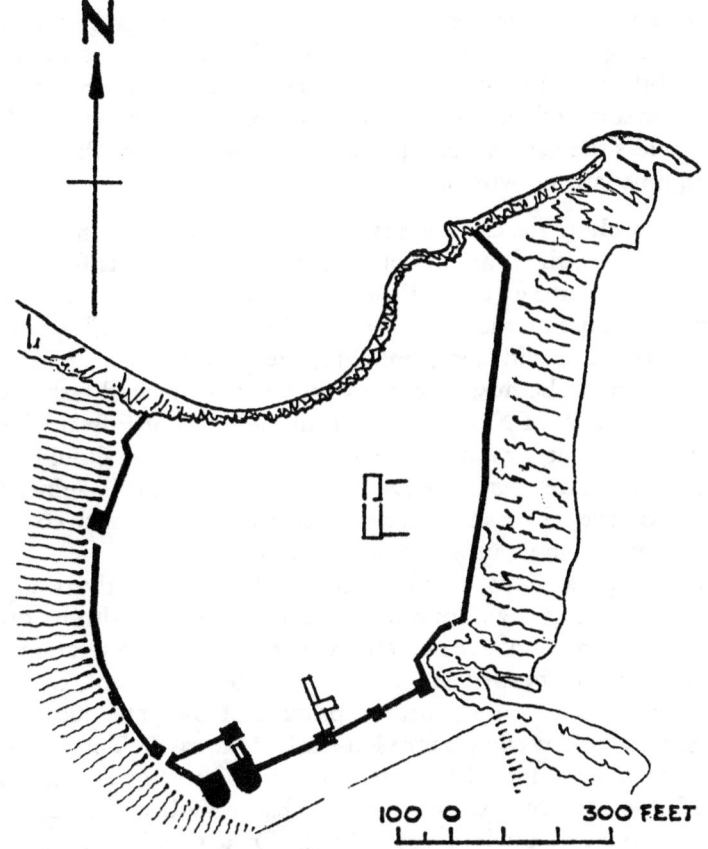

FIG. 24. Dunstanburgh Castle: sketch plan.

planted on a sheer basalt cliff thrust forth against the North Sea. The historian Freeman has described it thus:

'Its isolated hill stands yet more nobly than the isolated hill of Bamburgh; the waves dash more immediately at its feet, boiling up in a narrow channel close under its walls, as if art and nature had joined together to make the fortress of Earl Thomas grim and awful above all other fortresses. Nothing can well be conceived more striking than the Lilburn Tower, a Norman keep in spirit, though far later in date, rising on the slope of the wild hill with the tall basaltic columns standing in front of it "like sentinels of stone". Yet, simply as a building, one is almost more struck if one approaches from the opposite side, and if the vast gateway, with its two huge circular towers, is the first feature to burst upon us. It doubtless has its rivals in other places where we more naturally look for some of the great works of human skill. In that desolate wilderness the gateway and the whole castle have an effect which is sublime beyond words.'[1]

Approaching the castle across the downs from the fishing hamlet of Craster, the long line of walls and towers looks for all the world like a fortified town. From far off one sees the towers of the keep-gatehouse on the left, of the usual round form, and the other towers on the grand front, stretching away to the right, all square. This is curious, because square towers were by now old-fashioned. The town walls of Newcastle, built in the reign of Edward I, are already of the new round pattern. Why Earl Thomas should have preferred square towers at Dunstanburgh I cannot imagine. He seems to have set a fashion; for in later castles in the north country the towers are more usually square than round.

The keep-gatehouse is greatly ruined, but was clearly arranged in the same way as at Tonbridge and Llanstephan, with its great hall on the *second* floor. And here the very same later alteration has been made. For between 1372 and 1383, John of Gaunt, Duke of Lancaster, built up the entrance passage of the gatehouse,[2] and constructed a new entry on the left flank of the castle. This brought a visitor directly into the great courtyard, on to a level area from which the keep or tower-house, as it had now become pure and simple, could readily be assailed. So the Duke shut it off by a small courtyard, enclosed by a wall and having a gateway protected by a square tower. Under this new arrangement, the former keep-gatehouse became a purely passive donjon in the old Norman

[1] E. A. Freeman, *English Towns and Districts*, pp. 329-30.
[2] This blocking, at both ends of the passage, has been removed in modern times.

style, placed at the rear of the new enclosure—a curious return to out-of-date ideas.

Many have wondered why Earl Thomas built this vast castle in a remote corner of the Northumbrian moorland. Clearly its enormous area was meant to give room for the countryfolk of the neighbourhood, who at that time were being sorely harried by the victorious Scots. No doubt also it was meant to house a garrison of the 'hobelars' or light-armed and lightly mounted moss-troopers so useful in Border warfare. Indeed we know that the castle was used for both these purposes. The new type of keep-gatehouse was most necessary for a castle which had to maintain a large standing garrison, composed of troops notorious for their rough ways, and which also had to admit within its gates, whenever necessary, disorganized mobs of refugees, among whom enemy agents could easily find their way.

Nor should we think of this mighty fortress as designed merely for a garrison of moss-troopers. During the years when it was building, Earl Thomas was in open conflict with his sovereign. Indeed in those days England was torn between two rival governments, of the King and the Prince of Lancaster. Each moved about through the country, attended by a vast household of retainers, and supported by his own forces; for Earl Thomas raised and kept in his pay a private army as numerous as the levies of the King. For these mercenaries, quarters had to be found, and no doubt the huge enclosure of Dunstanburgh Castle was intended to play its part.

A writer of that time has well described the unhappy state of England:

'Whatever pleased the King, the household of the Earl strove to overthrow. Whatever pleased the Earl, the King's household declared to be treasonable. And so, at the suggestion of the Devil, the households of the Earl and the King put themselves in the way, and would not allow their lords, by whom the land should have been defended, to be of one accord.'[1]

So the Scots had it all their own way on the Borders:

'And thereof came it that the fleering Scots
To England's high disgrace, have made this jig:

[1] William of Malmesbury, *Vita Edwardi II*, in *Chronicles of the Reigns of Edward I and II* (Rolls series), Vol. II, p. 224.

MORE ABOUT EDWARDIAN CASTLES

'"Maids of England, sore may you mourn
For your lemans you have lost at Bannocksburn,
  With a heave and a ho!
What weeneth the King of England
So soon to have won Scotland,
  With a rombelow!"'[1]

In those sad days, many must have been the refugees who found shelter within the far-flung walls of Dunstanburgh.

It is not impossible that Earl Thomas had even grander ideas in building his great northern castle. Its name shows that he intended to found a borough in dependence on the castle. In fact the borough is known to have been in existence, and of some importance, as early as 1326. It had a small harbour, which may still be traced, though it is now blocked with shingle. In 1514 an English squadron, on its way from Hull to the Firth of Forth, took shelter here. All this suggests that Earl Thomas planned to found a new town or *bastide* here, as a bulwark against the Scots, in the same way as his uncle, Edward I, and his father-in-law, Henry de Lacy, in North Wales.

There is another point of interest about Dunstanburgh. The great frontal wall with its array of towers is all built of finely dressed stone. But the wall along the cliff is roughly built of rubble work, and in the interior these stones are laid only in clay. Clearly the keep-gatehouse and the grand front are the work of a skilled architect. He was Master Elias, and we have a hint that he may have come from Wales. But the cliff wall looks more like the work of local builders. It is built in short sections, usually about forty feet long. The joints between different sections can be clearly seen. Probably this work was carried out by the Embleton tenantry, each one forced to do his own bit under the feudal obligation known as castle-work. These farmer-folk would be used to putting up their own steadings and fences, and would be well able, under supervision, to build this cliff wall at their castle.

The walls of the Roman town of Caerwent, in South Wales, were built in sections in the same way. So are some prehistoric forts in Ireland. There is another Roman instance of this manner of building at Pevensey Castle in Sussex. When the Children of Israel rebuilt the destroyed parts of the wall of Jerusalem, under

[1] Marlowe, *Edward II*, Act II, Sc. ii.

MORE ABOUT EDWARDIAN CASTLES

the direction of the prophet Nehemiah, the work was divided out among different gangs: 'So built we the wall; and all the wall was joined together with the half thereof; for the people had a mind to work.'

Consideration of three important castles—Tonbridge, Llanstephan, Dunstanburgh—has shown that the keep-gatehouse idea, though ingenious, turned out in practice to be not altogether a success. The attempt to combine a lord's residence with a fortified gatehouse did not work. And there are other instances which tell the same tale. At three Scottish castles, St. Andrew's and Macduff's, both in Fife, and Huntingtower in Perthshire, the passage in the tower of entry has been walled up, and a new one made alongside it. And there is at least one similar example in Ireland, at Roscrea Castle in County Tipperary.

NOTE

By the time of Edward I the old timber hoardings or war-heads on towers and walls were being replaced by permanent oversailing stone parapets carried forward on corbels. Between each pair of corbels was a hole through which offensive materials could be cast down upon assailants. Such holes are called machicolations. A machicolated parapet will be seen on Plates 9 and 11.

IX
The Tower of London: and Windsor Castle

THE Tower of London is the most complete example of a concentric castle, and Windsor is the largest British castle on the *motte* and bailey plan, so in this chapter it will be worth while to take a look at each of them.

During the troubles of King Stephen's reign, in 1153, there was an agreement to place the Tower of London and the *motte* of Windsor—*Turris Londonensis et Mota de Windesor*—in the custody of the Justiciar. It shows very clearly the difference between the two kinds of Norman castle.

The Tower stands in the south-east corner of the Roman city. Part of the Roman wall is still visible close east of the Norman keep, and Roman bricks were used occasionally inside the keep. This keep was founded by William the Conqueror, who began to build it in 1078. His purpose was partly to overawe the turbulent Londoners, and partly to protect them against the Danes, who repeatedly threatened England during the Conqueror's reign.

Probably the keep was not completed until the reign of William II. Its upper portions are not so well built as the lower. It was called the White Tower, because it was regularly whitewashed, a common practice for stone buildings in the Middle Ages.

Although it has been much pulled about, the White Tower remains the finest of Norman keeps. From the outset it must have been secured against the city by some kind of outer enclosure. No doubt at first this would take the form of a palisade. In fact, traces of this early defence have been discovered to the north of the Wakefield Tower. Later, in the usual way, stone walls replaced the stockade. This early courtyard was less than half the size of the present Inner Bailey. A considerable part of its west wall is still preserved, running north from the Wakefield Tower. The palace or great hall, with its attendant buildings, was on the river front, between the Wakefield and Lanthorn Towers. From this, the Wakefield Tower used to be called the Hall Tower. In this tower, opening off the hall, were the king's private rooms, including a beautiful little oratory which is still well preserved. This is 'the chapel in the new tower near the King's Hall, towards the Thames', mentioned in 1238. The Wakefield Tower is known to have been built in 1221. Much rebuilt at various times, the palace was finally removed by Cromwell.

It was under the Plantagenets that the Tower was extended to its present size, and became the earliest, as it is still the most complete, example in Britain of a concentric castle. The Exchequer Rolls tell us that work was in progress from the reign of Henry II, though it is not easy to form a clear idea of the successive stages. But the great outer ditch was dug by Richard I, and this shows that the fortress had already reached its present size; though the outer line of defence was probably still of timber. We learn that in 1194 a palisade, defended by mangonels or spring guns, was made 'about the Tower of London'. In a single year King Richard spent £2,881 on his works at the Tower, and this must represent a great amount of construction.

Next to the White Tower, the oldest surviving part of the castle is perhaps the lower part of the Bell Tower, at the south-west corner of the Inner Bailey. This may be the work of King Richard I.

But it is to Henry III and Edward I that we owe the existing double curtain wall which makes the Tower into a concentric castle. One of the grandest of the Crusading castles in Syria, Krak des Chevaliers, had been converted into a very complete concentric castle early in the thirteenth century; but it does not show anything corresponding to the splendid English keep-gatehouses.

A curious feature about the Tower is that while the inner and outer curtains are, for the most part, flanked by the round towers usual in the thirteenth century, there is a group of square towers at the east end of the Outer Bailey. There are now thirteen towers on the Inner Bailey: the Outer Bailey has six towers fronting the river, and on the opposite or north side are three large artillery bastions, probably replacing former towers. The whole castle, including the moat, covers not less than twelve acres.

In its final form, the Tower had two main entrances. One was from the river, through the famous Traitors' Gate. Its proper name is St. Thomas's Gate, from a chapel which it contained, dedicated to St. Thomas of Canterbury. Its great arch, 28 feet wide, spanned by a huge portcullis, enabled boats to be admitted into the tower. This contains a large basin, in which the water rose to a height of 8 feet at high tide. From this, steps lead up to the Bloody Tower, through which passes the entrance to the Inner Bailey. The inner face of the Traitors' Gate is carried on a more cleverly built arch. It has a span of 61 feet, and as the rise of the arch is only $15\frac{1}{2}$ feet, the builder evidently feared that it might not be strong enough. Therefore he made the arch stones each with a kink or notch, so that they are all locked in one to another. This is known as 'joggled' construction. Traitors' Gate was built in 1242.

The second entrance to the Tower gives access from the City of London. Plantagenet kings were constantly at loggerheads with the Londoners, and seeing the care with which they secured this entrance we can understand how much they feared the city mob. To the burghers, on their part, the Tower was always 'London's lasting shame'. So the kings took no risks in providing for the defence of the approaches from the city.

First of all on Tower Hill, there was a barbican. This has now disappeared. From it, the approach led to the outer gatehouse, known as the Middle Tower, on the far side of the great moat. The entrance here was strongly secured, and defended by two round towers.

Beyond the Middle Tower, a long wooden bridge gave access across the moat to the inner gatehouse, the Byward Tower. This is like the Middle Tower, only larger. It contains living-rooms on the upper floors, but there is no great hall, neither do there seem to have been a rear portcullis and a rear gate closing against the bailey. So we cannot class the Byward Tower as a keep-gatehouse. In its upper rooms, some very beautiful wall and ceiling paintings have recently been discovered. These date from the fourteenth century. They remind us that the interiors of the Tower of London, now so grey and drab, in the brave days of old were bright with colour. For example, in the time of Henry III the Queen's Chamber was painted white, with a pattern of roses.

The inner outlet of the Byward Tower is commanded from the rear by the strong Bell Tower at the south-west corner of the Inner Bailey. The lower part of this tower is multangular, but it becomes round above. From this point the approach continues along between the outer and inner curtains to the Bloody Tower.

Of all the ancient buildings that once crowded the Inner Bailey, only two now survive. One is the King's House, built for his private lodging by Henry VIII, and now used by the Resident Governor of the Tower. It is a charming example of half-timber work; the walls framed with large timbers, the spaces between filled in with lath and plaster.

The other ancient building that survives in the Inner Bailey is the Chapel Royal, otherwise known as the Chapel of St. Peter *ad vincula*. This means St. Peter in chains, and the chapel is so called after a church in Rome, where chains said to have been used to bind the Apostle are shown yearly on his festival day, August 1st. The Chapel Royal is first mentioned in 1210, but the present building was erected by Henry VIII. The Chapel Royal has been described as the saddest place in all England, because of the number of noble and distinguished victims of royal justice or royal malice who sleep within its walls. In the crypt are said to lie the remains of no less than sixty-three people, all but nine of whom died by the headsman's axe.

Of course, additions and alterations have continued to be made to the buildings in the Tower right down until our time. But the final scheme seems to have been completed by the reign of Edward I; and the last stage may be thought to have been reached in 1287 when that king enlarged the moat. This is now between 30 and 40 yards in width. It was supplied with water from the Thames, which flowed in at high tide and during the ebb was kept in by sluices. But as the Thames water was just as dirty then as it is now, and since besides much filth was cast into it from the Tower, the stench of the moat became appalling. Nevertheless this did not prevent the Cockneys from bathing in it. So Edward III decreed that the penalty for anyone caught bathing in the Tower ditch was death—though one might rather think it would have been death to bathe in it!

If the Tower of London is reminiscent of much that is stern and cruel in the history of the English monarchy, Windsor Castle represents its medieval glories. I think this is the grandest of all British castles (see Plate 6).

Windsor is probably the greatest castle in Europe designed upon the mount-and-bailey plan. Its two enormous baileys, on either side of the central *motte*, appear both to have been laid out at the same time, and by William the Conqueror, the founder of the castle. The whole area enclosed by them is not less than 13 acres.

As usual, the Conqueror's vast earthworks were defended by palisades. So far as we know, it was Henry II who began to replace these with stone walls and towers. Considerable parts of his work, though much altered and mostly refaced, still remain, particularly in the eastern or Upper Ward. According to the fashion of the time, his towers were square. The lower part of the shell wall round the *motte* is also his building. The name of the royal engineer who carried out these mighty works was Ailnoth, and his salary was £10 12s. 11d. a year.

Henry II also built himself a stone dwelling-house against the north wall of the Upper Ward. Much of this work still remains in the basement of the present royal apartments.

In 1216, during the civil war between King John and his barons, Windsor Castle was besieged and much damaged by battering engines. Repairs on a large scale were undertaken by Henry III, who completed the walling round the western or Lower Ward. His towers were of the new semi-circular form. They can best be studied on the western front of the castle, where three fine towers and their connecting curtains still remain in wonderful preservation. These are the Clewer or Belfry Tower, Garter's Tower, and the Chancellor's Tower. The towers have all been refaced in modern times, but the curtain walls are little altered. They are well built of small squared stones laid in courses, with horizontal bands of larger and lighter-coloured ashlars. It is similar to the kind of masonry afterwards used by Edward I at Caernarvon Castle.

This is the only part of Windsor where anything of the great outer ditch still remains. This ditch is not Norman, for the Conqueror's ditch lay further back. In fact, Henry III's three towers and curtain walls are built in the earlier ditch, and the ditch we now see in front of them is Henry's work. To make it, he had to clear away some houses belonging to 'honest men of Windsor', who were paid £7 5s. for the loss of their homes.

In spite of modern alterations, I do not know anything that will give a better idea of an ancient castle as a going concern than this western front of Windsor.

King Henry also rebuilt the royal lodgings in the Upper Ward, and the Norman great hall and its attendant kitchen and chambers in the Lower Ward. Here also he constructed a chapel with a cloister on its north side. Part of this cloister walk still remains. It is one of the most beautiful things in the castle. In the Queen's chamber in the royal lodging a stained-glass window, depicting the Tree of Jesse, was put up in the year 1236. And in 1251 the dais windows of the Great Hall in the Lower Ward were likewise fitted with painted glass. On 17 June 1239 a prince, afterwards King Edward I, was born to Queen Eleanor; and on 11 August following, the King ordered a nursery to be fitted up for the royal infant. How vividly such records bring back to mind the family life of Plantagenet kings in Windsor Castle, more than seven centuries ago!

What is nowadays called redundancy in labour was dealt with in King Henry's time after a fashion which modern trade unions would much dislike. Here is a curious order sent down by the King to Windsor Castle on 23 November 1252:

'Because there are many more workmen in the Castle of Windsor than is necessary, from whose works by reason of the shortness of the days of this present time the King derives little profit, the King wills that the greater part of them be discharged, together with the painters who are in the same castle, whom the King wills to cease from their works for a season since they cannot work properly by reason of the dampness of winter time. And the Constable of Windsor is ordered to discharge from the castle the greater part of the aforesaid workmen, as may seem expedient, together with those painters, until the King order otherwise.'[1]

By the close of King Henry's reign the Castle of Windsor had become, so a writer of those days proudly declares, 'that very

[1] Sir Wm. H. St. John Hope, *Windsor Castle*, Vol. I, pp. 39-40.

flourishing castle, than which at that time there was not another more splendid within the bounds of Europe'.[1]

So far as the outer walls are concerned, the principal later addition is the splendid gateway in the Lower Ward, built by Henry VIII probably in 1510–11. Its two towers have three-sided fronts. This was probably the last great castle gatehouse to be built in England. But there is no great hall in its upper part, neither has there been a portcullis in the inner or courtyard side. So this is not a keep-gatehouse of the Edwardian type.

Of the numerous and splendid buildings which now surround both the courtyards it is impossible for me to write anything in this book. They have to be visited. But something must be said about the Chapel of St. George, in the Lower Ward. This is the place of worship of the proudest English Order of Chivalry, the Knights of the Garter, founded by Edward III in 1348.

The present Chapel was begun by Edward IV, and finished about 1497 by Henry VII. It is perhaps the finest example of the Perpendicular style of Gothic architecture. This style is found only in England, and its flourishing period was the fifteenth century—though it was used much later, and indeed many modern churches and public buildings have been put up in this style. It can be recognized from the way in which the shafts of the tracery, by which the large windows are divided, run up stiffly and perpendicularly right to the top of the arches.

In this noble church the stalls of the Knights of the Garter, each with his helmet, banner and emblazoned coat of arms, make a magnificent display. No other church in Britain, save only Westminster Abbey, contains so many art treasures. It is the present burial place of the British royal family. Here lie Henry VI, Edward IV, Henry VIII, Charles I, George III, Edward VII, George V, and George VI, as well as many other members of the Tudor, Stewart and Hanoverian dynasties. Here also is the cenotaph of the Prince Imperial, the only son of Napoleon III. He was killed in an ambush in the Zulu War of 1879.

The present external aspect of Windsor Castle is familiar to all the world. Yet it is largely modern; for it is due to the very drastic restoration carried out early in the last century by two architects,

---

[1] *Flores Historiarum* (Rolls series), Vol. II, p. 481.

James Wyatt and his nephew, Sir Jeffry Wyatville, who were engaged successively by George III and George IV to convert what was then a rambling and neglected old castle into a well-planned and stately modern palace. This they very certainly did, though in the process they swept away many ancient buildings which today we would gladly see back again. Much more destruction of old work was carried out during the reign of Victoria. But today things are different, and all that still remains of the work of the Middle Ages at Windsor Castle is carefully preserved, and shielded from decay.

Sir Jeffry Wyatville's reconstruction of Windsor Castle is an impressive example of the Gothic Revival. In the eighteenth cencentury people regarded the art and architecture of the Middle Ages as barbarous and gave it the name Gothic. Latin and Greek were the literatures chiefly studied by educated men and women; and when they wanted to build a town mansion or country house, they chose the style of Greek or Roman architecture. So far did they carry their admiration of the ancient world, that when they wished to paint a portrait of some famous person, or put up a statue to him, they dressed the poor man in Roman costume or armour. So in the Upper Ward of Windsor Castle there is a bronze statue of Charles II, dressed in the armour of a Roman Emperor.

By the end of the eighteenth century people grew tired of this imitation of the literature and art of Greece and Rome. They began to turn with interest to the romantic history of their own land, and to its monuments, the churches and castles. This Romantic Revival was helped by such writers as Goethe and Schiller in Germany, and Scott in Britain. Indeed it was *Ivanhoe*, perhaps more than any other single book, that touched off the new fashion in England for the history and monuments of the Middle Ages. In architecture the new spirit led to the abandonment of Greek and Roman models and the revival of the native Gothic. Unhappily Gothic architecture was as yet little understood, since for years no one had paid much attention to it. So some of the early efforts of the Gothic revival are not nowadays greatly admired.

In particular, Wyatville's remodelling of Windsor Castle has been much criticized. Yet it remains an outstanding achievement for its time. One splendid thing he did was to heighten Henry II's shell wall round the *motte*, and so to create the Round Tower which now dominates Windsor.

It is often worth while to compare the plans of different castles.

Looking again at the plan of Caernarvon Castle (Fig. 19), one is struck by the curious form of the Upper Ward, which bulges out into a rounded or oval shape. At first sight, there is nothing in the configuration of the ground which accounts for this strange bag-shaped outline of the Upper Ward. Certainly it has no military reason. In fact, from the point of view of defence it was a disadvantage; for the way in which the Granary Tower sticks out prevented either the King's Gatehouse at the west end of the Upper Ward, or the North-East Tower at its eastern end, from properly flanking the north front of the Upper Ward between them. In fact, the North-East Tower had almost no flanking value at all—so little that the designer of the castle hardly bothered to provide this tower with bowslits.

The reason is that the present stone castle of Caernarvon was not the first building on the site. It occupies the position of a Norman castle on the *motte* and bailey plan. The *motte* stood on the ground now contained by the Upper Ward. James of St. George, Edward I's great architect, built the walls and towers of the Upper Ward round the *motte*. Hence the reason for its bulging outline. The *motte* in fact survived until as late as about the year 1870, and there still exists a photograph showing that it occupied practically all the Upper Ward.

The King and his architect could easily have removed the *motte* if they had wished to do so; but there is evidence which shows what Edward and his architect had in mind when they retained the old Norman *motte* and built their Upper Ward round about it. On all sides except towards the town (where the castle is guarded by a moat) there is an enormous outspreading apron of stone along the base of the walls. It is shown very clearly in Plate 5.

This remarkable stone apron, a kind of continuous buttress, can have been intended for no other purpose but to resist the outward pressure exerted on the new stone walls by the huge earthen mass of the *motte* inside. But the *motte* had been then in existence for two hundred years. By now the earth must have been thoroughly consolidated, and there was surely no reason to believe it would spread out further and push over or break the massive stone walls now built around it. The only reason why King Edward's builders put this huge apron round the walls with which they enclosed the *motte* must be that they intended to crown the *motte* with a heavy stone tower, and that they feared the weight of this might cause the artificial earthen mound to slip—which is just what happened at Duffus Castle in Morayshire.

This should be compared with Windsor, where the earthen *motte*, crowned by the mighty Round Tower, dominates the castle and gives character to its appearance, as seen from every side, far or near. Caernarvon Castle was intended not only to be a great fortress and the seat of government for Wales, but also a royal palace, the residence of the Prince of Wales. Clearly this is the reason why Caernarvon Castle is so ornate a building, whereas Edward's other Welsh castles are severely plain. It cannot be doubted that at Caernarvon the King intended to create a second smaller Windsor. With its Lower and Upper Wards, each enclosed by a great array of walls and towers, and the Norman *motte* crowned by a great stone tower overlooking the whole, Caernarvon Castle, had the great King's design been realized, would indeed have been the Windsor of Wales.

Years ago I excavated the buried castle of Coull in Aberdeenshire, which had been held for England during the occupation of Scotland by Edward I. Thereafter it disappears entirely from history; it was probably captured and destroyed by the Scots in the course of the campaign in Aberdeenshire in 1308, when all the castles held by the English in that part of Scotland were recaptured by King Robert Bruce or his adherents.

When we dug Coull Castle we found every sign that it had been violently destroyed. The walls and towers lay overthrown, and the wooden buildings inside had been set on fire. In front of the gateway was a deep pit, cut in the living rock, and this had been spanned by a wooden bridge. In the pit we found the burnt timbers of the bridge, with scores of nails, many melted or partly melted by the heat. We even found the ash of the fascines or bundles of brushwood which had been used to fire the bridge.

When we came to the main sewer of the principal tower of the castle, we found it choked with filth. This suggested to us that the castle had fallen after a siege or close blockade, during which the garrison had been unable to get outside to clean out their drains.

In the course of our excavations, we obtained a large haul of relics. This was chiefly because we were lucky enough to come across several of the middens upon which the inmates of the castle had thrown out their refuse. Among our finds were quantities of potsherds; and the date which can be assigned to this pottery is in entire agreement with the idea that Coull Castle had been destroyed by the Scots in the campaign of 1308.

One little scrap of painted ware that we found puzzled me greatly. It was quite unlike all the rest of the pottery. At the time I could make nothing of it. Years afterwards, when the polychrome ware about which I have mentioned earlier turned up at Kidwelly Castle, my sherd from Coull was looked at again by experts. They said it was not the same as the polychrome ware—which probably came with the wine trade from Bordeaux; but the Coull piece was declared to be what is known as Orvieto ware, from central Italy. Here and in this neighbourhood in the thirteenth and fourteenth centuries a great deal of painted pottery, of the type known to collectors as majolica ware, was manufactured. Probably the little sherd is a fragment of the rim of a drug jar.

It will be remembered that Edward I was always in money difficulties. His troubles came to a head in 1292. He had promised to lead a Crusade, and for this purpose an Italian banking firm, the Ricciardi, had advanced him the huge sum of 100,000 crowns, £66,666. Now Edward suddenly found himself involved in two outbreaks of war at once: a rising in Wales and an attack by the French King upon his possessions in Gascony. On top of all this came the disputed succession in Scotland. Faced with all these troubles, and at his wits' end to find ready cash to pay his troops, the King seized upon this money which had been advanced to him for his Crusade. To satisfy his Italian bankers, Edward made them assignations, grants of the revenues of Crown lands—including many baronies that had fallen into his hands as lord paramount of Scotland. Among the rents so assigned by the hard-pressed King were certain sums due on account of the barony of Aboyne, to which at that time the castle of Coull was attached.

Now the banking firm of the Ricciardi had their headquarters at Lucca, which is close to Orvieto and in the heart of the majolica

9. Bodiam Castle: aerial view from the South
   (See pp. 117-20)

10. Doune Castle: general view from the North-East
(See pp. 122-4)

country; and the London agent of the firm, Nicholas de Colle, came from a town in the same area. It was to him that Edward assigned the sums due him from the barony of Aboyne. In accordance with the practice of those times, Nicholas would have to travel round himself, or send an agent round on his behalf, collecting the moneys which had been assigned to his firm from various lands in Scotland. It looks as if he or one of his men must have visited Coull, then the chief castle in the barony of Aboyne, bringing with him among his medical stores a drug jar made in his province. The jar, we may suppose, got broken, and was thrown out upon the castle midden.

Such evidence can be more attractive than guide-books, but it is unwise to dig without proper knowledge and authority.

X
Northern Tower-Houses

Two miles west from Peterborough there is a remarkable little castle, or fortified manor-house, called Longthorpe Tower. It is an ancient property of the Thorpe family, and stands in the village of Longthorpe, close beside the village church, which we know was built after the lord of the manor, William de Thorpe, had received in 1264 a licence from the Abbot of Peterborough to provide himself with a private chapel on his grounds. William de Thorpe's residence forms the oldest part of Longthorpe Tower, and as its windows closely resemble those of the parish church, it is doubtless of about the same date.

It was a hall-house of quite modest dimensions. The hall, as usual, was on the first floor, with storage below. No doubt there were other buildings—kitchen, solar, and so forth. Some remnants of these may survive in the wings of the present house, but these seem to be of much later date. The walls are thin, and the house may have been quite unfortified; there are no traces of an encircling wall or moat.

But early in the fourteenth century, probably in the reign of Edward II, there was added to this undefended little mansion a massive tower-house, at least 40 feet in height, and measuring 26 feet square over the walls, which are no less than six or seven feet thick. The two lower storeys are vaulted and were therefore fireproof. The basement contains a cellar, entered from the store beneath the old hall, but having no communication with the floor above. This floor, opening from the old hall, provided a solar or private room for the lord. It is well fitted up, with good windows, a fireplace, and a privy. All four sides of this room are decorated with a magnificent series of contemporary wall-paintings, among the finest of their kind in Western Europe. They were discovered when Longthorpe Tower, occupied by the Home Guard during the war, was being reconditioned.

The floor above, which is unvaulted, contained the lord's bedroom. It has good windows and a privy, but there is no fireplace. Presumably the owner kept himself warm at night with a brazier. Over all, the tower has an open embattled parapet, commanding a wide view across the Nene valley.

Now the addition, about the year 1325, of a strong defensive tower to an unfortified mansion in peaceful East Anglia, is a surprising thing. The tower is in fact a miniature Norman keep. But we have seen that such strong rectangular towers were going out of fashion in England a full century and a half before this one at Longthorpe was built. Why did the lord of Longthorpe suddenly fortify his manor-house in this formidable way?

It is significant that the valley of the Nene has been from early times a waterway from the east coast of England into the Midlands. I imagine, therefore, that the tower was built during the French war which began in 1324 and ended three years later with the landing of Queen Isabella at Orwell in Suffolk and the downfall of poor Edward II. The public records of those days tell much about the defensive measures which were taken at that time all along the southern and eastern coasts.

Nowhere in Britain is it possible to see more clearly how the interior of a medieval house looked in its original state. The rooms which look so gaunt in ruined castles were once bright with glowing colours. The pictures at Longthorpe form a wonderful series. Some are sacred in character, others have a moral like Aesop's fables, others again are scenes from the romances of chivalry. One very fine series of figures round the arch of a window shows the Twelve Labours of the Months. Unfortunately only five of these figures are preserved. January is warming himself with a blazing fire and a bowl of soup. February has already started working in the fields. March is digging hard with a large spade. April is a young man holding a posy of flowers. All the others are destroyed except December, who is a butcher killing a pig.

There is another series displaying the Seven Ages of Man. For example, Infancy is shown as a baby asleep in its cradle. Boyhood is a lad with a whipping top. Youth is out on a hawking expedition. Old Age, bent and hollow-cheeked, hobbles on crutches and tries to keep himself warm in a long hooded cloak.

Among the sacred scenes, one has been a fine painting of the Nativity but it is now badly damaged. A number of the Apostles are shown at various places: St. Peter, St. Paul, St. Andrew, St. James. There is a picture of King David playing on his harp. Other musical instruments carried by figures in some of the subjects include bagpipes and a portable organ.

A grimmer note is sounded by a picture of the Three Living Kings and the Three Dead Kings. The latter are shown as skeletons or as corpses being devoured by worms. But perhaps the most striking subject is the Wheel of the Five Senses. A king is shown turning the wheel, on the rim of which are perched a spider, a boar, a cock, a monkey and a vulture. The spider symbolizes touch, the boar hearing, the cock sight, the monkey taste, and the vulture smell. All this was explained by inscriptions painted on the rim and spokes of the wheel. Why a king should be shown as turning the wheel is not quite clear. Perhaps he is intended for Reason controlling the senses. The king looks extremely sad, so perhaps the painter had not much faith in the ultimate triumph of Reason.

The artist of the Longthorpe paintings was evidently a bird-lover. Charming pictures of birds appear at various places in the paintings: a peacock, a goose, an owl, a magpie, a bittern. There is also a delightful little picture of a squirrel sitting up gaily and eating a nut.

The artist well knew how decorative is the science of heraldry: coats of arms, once brightly tinctured, splendidly adorned this room. They include the arms of King Edward II and his uncle, the Earl of Kent, with their portraits, though that of the Earl has been almost destroyed.

Longthorpe Tower was a remarkable thing to have been erected in East Anglia during the reign of Edward II; but in the three northern counties of England, scene of so many devastating invasions by the Scots, such a tower-house would have aroused no surprise. Indeed it became the most familiar feature of the landscape there during the fourteenth and fifteenth centuries. The northern tower-houses were not great royal castles or the strongholds of mighty feudal lords, but mansions of the smaller landowners, the country gentry. They are utterly different from the kind of house in which these people had been living before Edward I's disastrous attack upon Scotland.

One of the most interesting of ancient houses in the north of England is Aydon Castle, near Hexham in Northumberland. It stands in a romantic situation on a bold bluff within a loop of the Aydon Burn, which hurries down a deep tree-lined glen on its way to join the Tyne. The castle is quite close to the old Roman town of Corbridge. As first built, it was simply a stone version of the early form of hall-house which was described in the first chapter of this book; with a central hall, the kitchen at its lower end and the solar, or lord's private suite, forming a crossbar at the upper end like the letter T. The house was built towards the end of the thirteenth century, and in its original form was completely unfortified. But then came the long wars with Scotland, and we have the owner's description of what they caused him to do with Aydon Hall. Writing in 1315, Robert de Raymes reports that 'he had lately fortified his dwelling house at Aydon with a wall of stone and lime against the King's enemies, the Scots'. It was the year after Bannockburn; moreover in 1312 the Scots had burned both Hexham and Corbridge, and laid waste the whole countryside. Those were the black years when the weakness of Edward II and his devotion to Piers Gaveston had lost Scotland and yielded up Northumberland to the invaders:

> 'Unto the walls of York the Scots made road,
> And unresisted drave away rich spoils.
>
> The northern borderers seeing their houses burnt,
> Their wives and children slain, run up and down,
> Cursing the name of thee and Gaveston.'[1]

The wall which Robert de Raymes then built still remains. It is strong and thick, with a square and a round flanking tower, and encloses a large courtyard, protecting the house on all sides except the south, where the steep bank of the Aydon Burn makes an

[1] Marlowe, *Edward I*, Act II, Sc. ii.

NORTHERN TOWER-HOUSES

attack unlikely. On the one side where there was no natural slope, a broad and deep ditch was dug outside the new curtain wall.

But this was not the first step that had been taken to strengthen Aydon Hall. Ten years earlier, in 1305, the owner had received a royal licence to fortify his house. The verb used in such a licence was to crenellate. Crenellations were the battlements on top of a wall, which enabled it to be defended. As a result of that licence, the lord of Aydon had built, in front of his house, a thick wall with a well-defended door, enclosing a small square courtyard. The crenellations, just as they had been sanctioned by royal licence, still remain on the wall-top. Like those at Caernarvon Castle, the embrasures are fitted with swinging shutters to protect the bowmen, and the merlons are pierced with slits for observation purposes. When the second and larger curtain wall was added, before 1315, this crenellated wall of 1305 became an inner bailey to what had now grown into quite a large and strong castle. Ten years of war had turned the Hall into Aydon Castle.

Yet all his expenditure in stone and lime did not avail poor Robert de Raymes when the Scots burst into Northumberland in the spring of 1315. Although the castle was well stocked with munitions and provisions, the captain, a Welshman named Hugh, betrayed it to the invaders, who sacked the place and burnt it.

If Aydon had been in the south of England, the original hall-house would probably have been built of half-timber work. Being in Northumberland it was built in stone, and so were the later curtain walls. Subsequent owners were never wealthy and could not afford to rebuild or enlarge it. So Aydon Hall or Aydon Castle —both names are still in use—remains the most perfect example of a fortified manor-house. The original hall-house, erected in times of peace, is beautifully built of dressed stonework, with lovely Gothic details. The walls added in the years of war are not so finely built.

Aydon shows how a peaceful country house in Northumberland had to be fortified to meet the perils of the Scottish wars. During this violent time, when a new house was designed, it had to be built as a strong fortalice. For such a need, in the case of a squire of moderate means, the plan of a simple rectangular tower was clearly both the cheapest and the most convenient. So wild were the times that even the parish priests had to desert their quiet rectories or vicarages and house themselves in strong square

NORTHERN TOWER-HOUSES

towers. At Corbridge, close beside the ancient parish church, is a fine example of such a vicar's tower.

The tower is small but strong, and many stones from the Roman town have been used in its walls. It has three storeys, each of a single room; the lowest is vaulted and was the vicar's cellar. On the first floor was his parlour, or living-room, and above was his study-bedroom. A door on the ground floor leads directly into the cellar, which is lit only by two narrow slits. The door is of wood, but plated with iron so as to be fireproof.

Beside the door a straight stair in the thickness of the wall leads up to the vicar's room. At the head of this stair is a stone wash-hand basin. The parlour has been quite a comfortable little room, with a good fireplace and windows with stone seats. There are also a privy and a couple of wall presses. The end of the hall which contains these cupboards has a small loophole to itself. I think therefore that this part of the hall was shut off by a wooden partition to form what in a Scotch tower would be called a 'spence', or inner storeroom. Sir Walter Scott described such a spence in his account of the Tower of Glendearg, in *The Monastery*.

A second stair inside the wall leads to the vicar's study-bedroom. This is much plainer, with no fireplace and only three small windows. But it has a stone book-rest, sloped at a convenient angle. So there was a comfortable hall for dispensing parish hospitality, but a study-bedroom was more in keeping with the self-denial that became a vicar's calling. One thinks of the priest of Chaucer:

> 'A good man was ther of religioun
> And was a povre PERSOUN of a town:
> But rich he was of holy thoght and werk.
> He was also a lerned man, a clerk,
> That Cristes gospel trewely wolde preche
> His parisshens devoutly wolde he teche.'[1]

Over all, the little tower is crowned by a defensive parapet, with square turrets at the four corners. The embrasures were fitted with swinging shutters as at Aydon. Corbridge was thrice burnt by the Scots in the Wars of Independence:

'Corbridge is a town, they brent it when they came.' So it was no excess of caution that drove the vicar to provide himself with

[1] *Canterbury Tales*, Prologue, 477-82.

a hideout in this stout defensive tower. At least one family in the borough had a similar house or fence—a tower which still forms the oldest part of the house now called Low Hall. In the opening chapter of *The Monastery* Scott has described this system of Border village defence:

'In each village or town were several small towers, having battlements projecting over the side walls, and usually an advanced angle or two with shotholes for flanking the doorway, which was always defended by a strong door of oak studded with nails, and often by an exterior grated door of iron.[1] These small peel houses were ordinarily inhabited by the principal feuars and their families: but, upon the alarm of approaching danger, the whole inhabitants thronged from their own miserable cottages, which were situated around, to garrison these points of defence. It was then no easy matter for a hostile party to penetrate into the village, for the men were habituated to the use of bows and firearms, and the towers being generally so placed that the discharge from one crossed that of another, it was impossible to assault any one of them individually.'

The phrase peel-tower or peel-house, by which these structures are known, comes from the Latin *palus*, a stake. It meant first the palisade by which such towers, if they stood in open country, were surrounded, to keep the assailants at a distance and provide a defensive enclosure for the owner's livestock. Later, the word began to be applied to the tower itself.

Tower-houses also became fashionable in Scotland. Here disorderly conditions, such as prevailed in the English border counties, continued throughout the whole country right down to the seventeenth century. So all the small lairds had to build themselves fortified houses, and for this no cheaper or more convenient form could be found than the plain rectangular tower. Thus the tower-house, in one form or another, became the characteristic type of the smaller Scottish castle from the time of the War of Independence onwards. In fact, no other nation has worked out the tower-house idea to a greater extent, or rung the changes upon it in such a variety of design.

[1] Usually, however, the iron gate was *inside* the wooden door. See below, p. 106.

NORTHERN TOWER-HOUSES

One has to imagine a tower-house province in Britain, north of the River Tees and including all Scotland and the four northern English counties. Ireland also forms a tower-house province. Disorderly conditions persisted there to an even greater degree than in Scotland, and the tower-house was the obvious answer to the small landowner's quest for security. Moreover, in Northern Ireland, which was settled by Scottish colonists in the reign of James VI and I, the new owners built many tower-houses of purely Scotch design.

As time went on it was usual for the owner of a peel-tower or peel-house to replace his palisade by a stone enclosing wall. This was called a barmkin, supposed to be a corruption of barbican. The whole scheme then became what was called a tower-house and barmkin. It is vividly brought before our eyes in this narrative of the capture of Lochwood Tower, in Annandale, in 1547:[1]

'We came there about an hour before day: and the greater part of us lay close without the barmkin. But about a dozen of the men got over the barmkin wall, and stole close into the house within the barmkin, and took the wenches and kept them secure within the house till daylight. And at sunrise, two men and a woman being in the tower, one of the men rising in his shirt, and going to the tower head, and seeing nothing stir about, he called to the wench that lay in the tower, and bade her rise and open the tower door and call up them that lay beneath. She so doing and opening the iron door, and a wooden door without it, our men within the barmkin brake a little too soon to the door. For the wench, perceiving them, leaped back into the tower, and had gotten almost the wood door to. But we got hold of it [so] that she could not get it close to. So the skirmish rose, and we over the barmkin and broke open the wood door. And she being troubled with the wood door left the iron door open: and so we entered and won the Lochwood!'

This account of a Border raid is from one who took part in it. Lochwood Tower consisted of three parts: there was the barmkin wall; inside the barmkin, probably built against the wall, was a house, containing a hall, kitchen, and stables, in which serving

[1] J. Nicolson and R. Burn, *History and Antiquities of the Counties of Westmorland and Cumberland*, Vol. I, p. liv.

women slept by night; and in the centre of the courtyard was the tower. Its entrance was defended first by a wooden door, and then by an iron gate. This was the usual arrangement. If the wooden door was burnt or broken up, the iron gate behind could not be destroyed in this way, and the defenders could shoot out between the bars. The iron gate was immediately behind the wooden door, so the door could not be opened until the gate had been unbolted and swung back. Both door and gate are well preserved still in some of the Scottish castles.

In England, such gates are made with the vertical bars all passing in front of the horizontal ones, and the whole is boarded on the inner side. The Vicar's Tower at Corbridge has an excellent example. In Scotland the iron gates are known as 'yetts'. They are of open iron work, without any boarding, and are formed in an ingenious way. The bars pass through each other, and the way of penetration is reversed in diagonally opposite quarters. The illustration (Plate 16) shows this arrangement clearly. The iron gratings which protect the windows of old Scottish castles are made in the same way.

Eventually the owners of such tower-houses began to want something more convenient than a dwelling of rooms arranged one on top of the other like a pile of biscuit boxes. A common way of getting extra space was to build the tower with a wing attached to the end of one side—like the letter L. This would give the owner at least one extra room on each floor. Often it gave him more; for the chambers in the wing, being usually private apartments, did not need to be so lofty as the halls or public rooms in the main house. So in an L-tower there are often five or even six storeys of small, low rooms in the wing, corresponding to four storeys in the main building.

Another plan was to use the wing for a spiral stair. In this way more convenient access was gained to the different parts of the main house, and the danger of weakening one of its angles by including a staircase was avoided.

One advantage of the L-plan was that it offered a very strong position for entrance to the tower. This could now be placed in the 're-entrant angle'—the hollow inner angle of the L, tucked away and screened by the projecting limbs of the building. In the

NORTHERN TOWER-HOUSES

plain rectangular towers the door is often placed, for security, on the first floor. Sometimes it is even on the second floor. But in the L-plan, owing to the strong position offered by the re-entrant angle, the door could be brought down to ground level. Of course this also was a notable gain in convenience.

This L-plan became a favourite type of tower-house in Scotland. Scores of examples are found up and down the country, many of them most cleverly arranged. A common plan was to put the main stair in the limb, but as far as the first floor only. Above this, the wing could then be made available for living-rooms; and both these and the upper floors of the main building could be served by a turret stair, corbelled out in the re-entrant angle.

There is a fine example of this kind of L-castle at Greenknowe Tower, in Berwickshire. Over the door is the date when it was built, 1581. Here also is a well-preserved yett of the characteristic Scottish design. With its overhanging turrets and crow-stepped gables, Greenknowe Tower (Plate 7) stands for this type of small Scottish house of fence of the reign of James VI.

Probably the finest of the northern English tower-houses are Chipchase and Belsay, both in Northumberland. Both were erected in the first half of the fourteenth century, and the resemblances between them are so close that it seems certain they were the work of the same architect. With their fat, round oversailing turrets, they have quite a Scottish appearance. Chipchase is still inhabited, while Belsay, though no longer occupied, is complete, and is kept in excellent order.

Chipchase Castle is built upon the L-plan. Its wing contains the entrance door and spiral stair, and is large enough to include a series of chambers, one above the other. The door was protected by a portcullis, an unusual feature in a simple tower-house. The basement of the main building contains a cellar. Above this is the common hall, then follows the lord's hall, and over all the solar, or lord's private apartment. In the wing at this level is a neat small kitchen—a most unusual feature, showing that already the lord of Chipchase was becoming tired of taking his meals in hall, and preferred to enjoy them with his family in their private room. The cooking for the general household must have been done in the barmkin, of which some portions remain.

NORTHERN TOWER-HOUSES

At Belsay Castle (Fig. 25) we find two wings, both on the same side of the tower. Thus the plan resembles the letter E, with the middle bar struck out. This gives a strong position to the entrance, in the recess between the two wings. It was thus protected on both

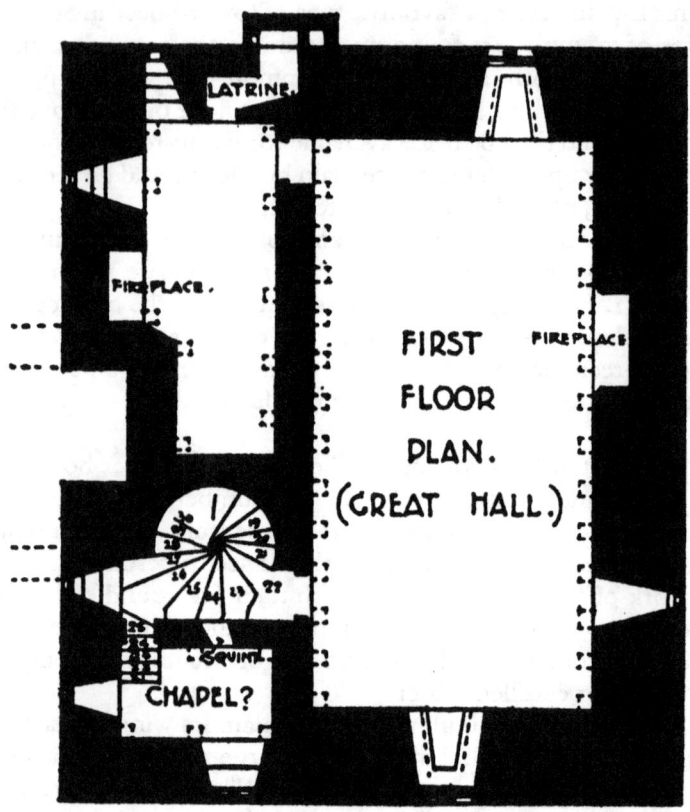

FIG. 25. Belsay Castle: first-floor plan.

flanks, and also from above by a timber hoarding which spanned the recess. The door being so well secured, no portcullis was provided at Belsay.

The southern wing contains the spiral staircase and, as at Chipchase, a series of small apartments. The northern wing is entirely occupied with living-rooms.

NORTHERN TOWER-HOUSES

On the first floor the main building contains the great hall, with a large fireplace and handsome windows having stone seats in their bays. The dais end of the hall is at the north end, and from here a door leads into the lord's private room, which occupied the northern wing. This has a fireplace and a latrine. From the stair in the southern wing a door opens into the screens end of the hall. At this level that wing also contains a small chamber, from which a service hatch opens on to the stair, close to the door into the hall. Although the little chamber has no fireplace, it otherwise resembles the small kitchen at Chipchase so exactly that there cannot be much doubt it was originally meant for the same purpose. (On the plan (Fig. 25) it is suggested that this little room might have been a chapel: but I think it is much more likely that it was originally a kitchenette.)

There is evidence that the building of Belsay Castle was interrupted, probably by the Black Death in 1349. Many building works, both in England and Scotland, were brought to a standstill because the craftsmen and labourers were dead. This is what seems to have happened at Belsay.

When work was resumed, it was evidently decided to have a much larger kitchen in the basement of the tower. One can see at a glance that the great arched fireplace here is an insertion. The original kitchenette was then turned into a little room. A window was cut out in what was probably the recess of the original fireplace. From the outside it is clear that this window is an afterthought.

If these interpretations are right, the architect had very cleverly gone back, in a *tower-house*, to the old horizontal arrangement of a *hall-house*, with the hall on the first floor, having the kitchen at the screens or lower end and the lord's room opening from the upper or dais end. This was the arrangement on the main floor of the great Norman keep at Newcastle-upon-Tyne (see above, p. 33).

By far the finest Scottish tower-house is Borthwick Castle in Midlothian. The royal licence to build was granted to Sir William Borthwick in 1430, and it is still inhabited. The castle is of great height, making a most imposing appearance with its heavy oversailing machicolated parapet. It is almost entirely fireproof, being stone-vaulted over all the principal rooms. The topmost vaults are pointed, and on these are laid the high-pitched, stone-slabbed roof. Outside and inside the walls are faced with beautiful squared stone. It has been calculated that there are no less than 13,000 tons of this

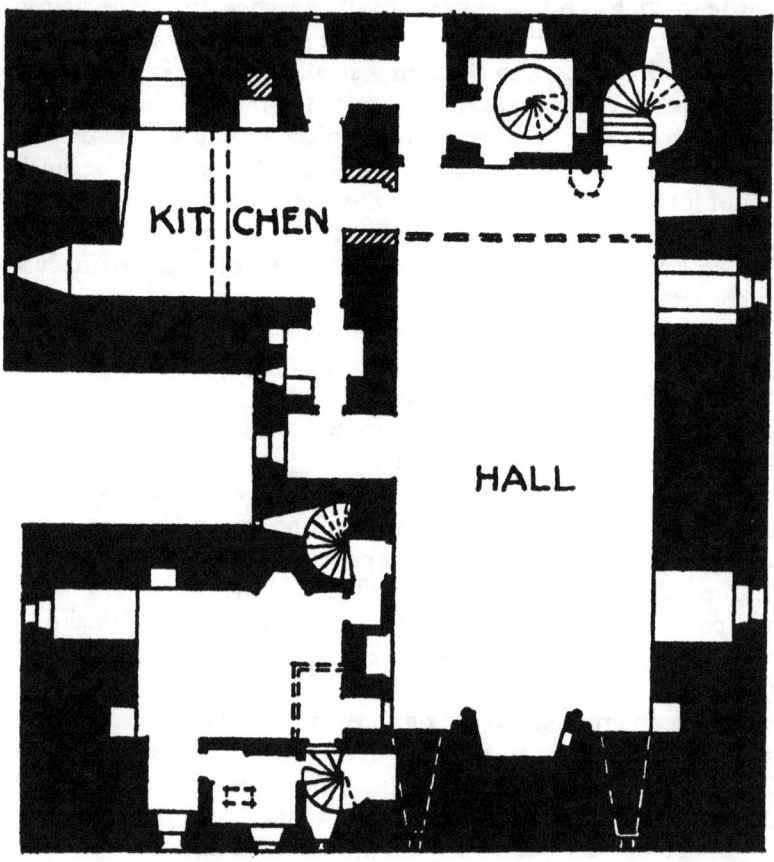

FIG. 26. Borthwick Castle: plan of first floor.

ashlar masonry in the castle, and that the whole building must weigh at least 30,000 tons.

Borthwick Castle, though much larger, is designed on the same plan as Belsay, with its central rectangular block and two wings,

NORTHERN TOWER-HOUSES

also rectangular, set out on one side. Unlike Belsay, however, the door is not in the recess between them.

The interior is much more elaborately planned than at Belsay, and has an astonishing number of rooms, stairs and passages. From the plan of the first floor (Fig. 26) it will be seen that the architect has used the two wings to obtain the same horizontal arrangement of kitchen, great hall and solar as at Belsay; though at Belsay the two wings mask the entire west side of the hall, where there can be no windows. On the other hand, at Borthwick the deep recess penetrates right back to the hall, and contains a window, so those in the hall can enjoy the western sun.

On 18 November 1650 that great pounder of castles, Oliver Cromwell, summoned Lord Borthwick to surrender. 'If you shall necessitate me to bend my cannon against you,'—so he wrote—'you must expect what I doubt you will not be pleased with.' That the Lord Protector was as good as his word can be seen to this day on the east wall of the castle. Here the parapet has been destroyed and a large area of the fine dressed stonework peeled off by the impact of round shot.

This chapter can end with two examples of the Scottish addiction to living in tower-houses. In 1644 Sir Alexander Innes of Coxton, the laird of a small estate near Elgin, completed a house for himself upon his property. There is evidence that his house may have been long a-building, or at least that much time was given to planning. His own coat of arms, and his wife's, are inside the building; but outside over the door are the coats of arms of his grandfather and of his two wives! The grandfather died in 1612, and presumably the outside stone was cut for him, but not dated and placed in position until the house was finished. As the date 1644 is carved on this stone, we may take that as the year in which the work was done. Sir Alexander, like his grandfather, was married twice. It is his first wife's coat of arms which appears alongside his own on the shield within the house. She died in 1647, so this stone must have been placed in position before that date. It is fairly certain that the date 1644 marks the completion of the house.

At a first glance (see Fig. 27) one might well imagine this to be a small tower of the fourteenth century. It is a simple square building of four storeys, with one room on each floor. The door is on the first floor, and was at first reached only by a ladder, though a

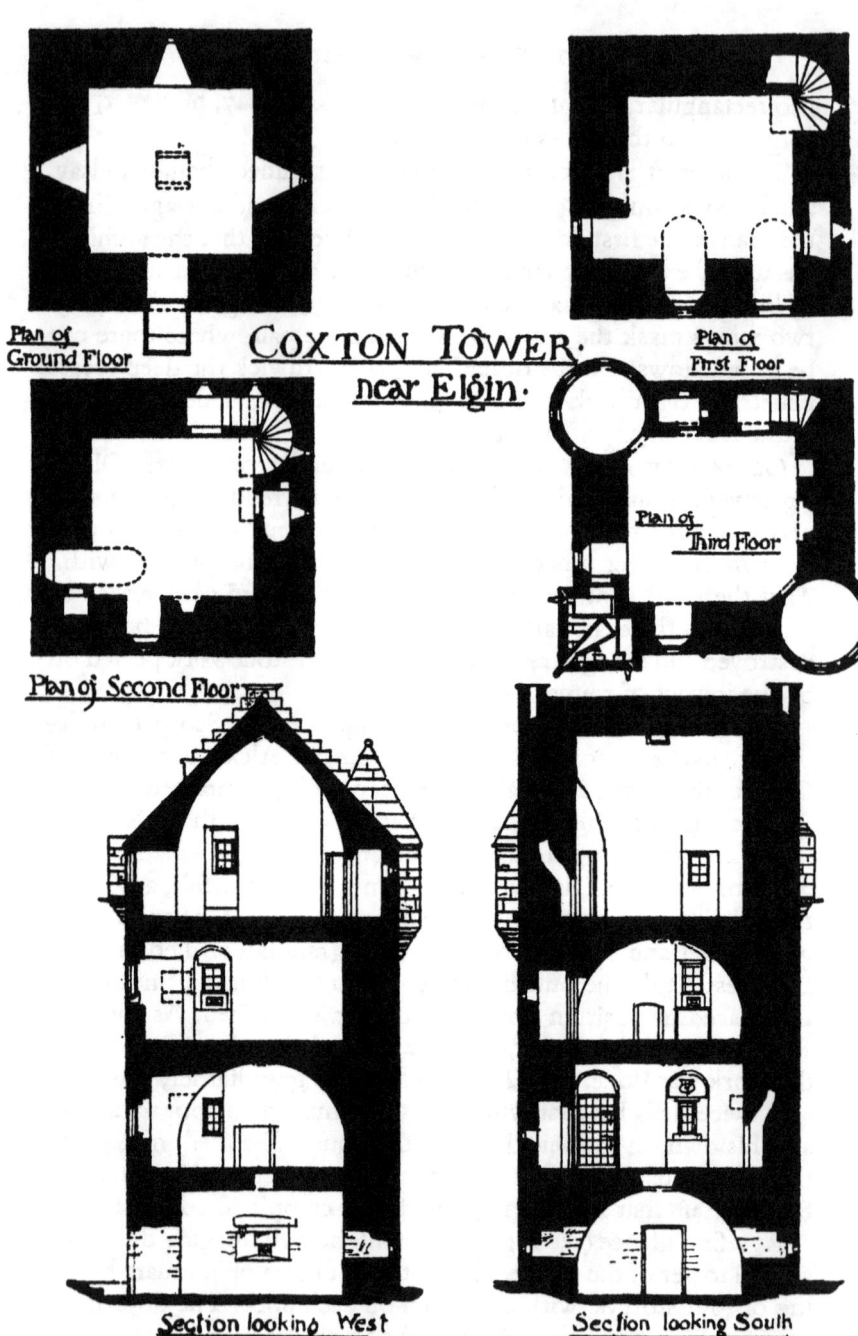

FIG. 27. Coxton Tower: plans and sections.

11. Tattershall Castle: view of great tower from South-West.
(See pp. 127-9)

12. Corfe Castle: general view from the South-East
(See pp. 137-41)

stone forestair has now been built up against it. All four rooms, one above the other, are vaulted. Now, had the axes of these vaults all been set the same way, the weight of all four would have rested on only two of the four walls of the tower. As the tower is 53 feet in height, and the walls, even on the ground level, are no more than 4 feet 6 inches thick, this weight of vaulting concentrated on only two of them might have split the little tower asunder; so the architect reversed the axis of each successive vault. The ground floor or cellar vault runs north and south, the vault over the hall runs east and west; the one over the solar goes north and south once more, and finally the vault over the uppermost room—the laird's bedchamber—runs east and west again.

So the weight of the vaults is spread equally over all the walls, and today there is not a crack to be seen in the little tower.

The only communication between the hall and cellar below is by a trap-door in the floor. As the stairs to the upper floors are narrow and inconvenient, there is in each floor a similar trap-door, so that stores could be hoisted up to each room in turn; it must have been a most uncomfortable arrangement.

All the floors, resting on vaults, are of course of stone. The uppermost vault is pointed and lofty, and on it are laid the stone slabs of the roof. Thus the whole tower is one solid mass of stone, and therefore completely fireproof. Except for the door and the window frames there is not a scrap of wood in it.

Inside the door is the usual iron yett, and the windows still have their iron gratings. In both yett and windows the bars intersect in the usual Scottish way.

On top of the tower are three angle turrets, two of which are round and capped by conical stone roofs like a candle extinguisher. The third turret is square and open to the sky, and between its corbels are machicolations. It thus forms a little post from which the door below could be defended. Also from this turret the laird could, if he wished, conduct a parley with attackers.

It is remarkable that such a tower could have been built so late as 1644, but all its architectural details—the style of its mouldings, the presence of gunloops or pistol-holes which are clearly original —show that the fortalice is really of the date it bears. The spouts that throw the rainwater off the open turret are carved like miniature cannon. It should be remembered that this tower-house was built at the height of the Civil War, during which Morayshire was the scene of bitter fighting. Nevertheless, it is an extraordinary thing that this 'bonnet laird'—as such small proprietors were called in Scotland—should build himself, in the first half of the seventeenth century, a tower-house that preserves unaltered the primitive arrangement of three centuries earlier, and with its fireproof construction, and its martial garniture of machicolations, gunloops and repelling ironwork, was obviously designed to withstand anything short of a bombardment.

Long after the fires of war had receded from Morayshire, this little tower continued to be occupied by its successive owners, without additions or improvements. The laird who died in it in 1708 was described by the family historian as 'one of the first gentlemen in Scotland, being a graceful person and one of fine natural parts'. So we have to think of one of the first gentlemen in Scotland, in the reign of Queen Anne, living in four rooms piled one on top of the other, in a tower to which his graceful person could obtain entrance only by climbing up a ladder!

No building in Scotland more startlingly exemplifies the long and stubborn native devotion to the tower-house as a suitable plan for a small laird's residence.

In 1658 the University authorities at King's College, Old Aberdeen, set themselves to build a new set of lodgings for their students, almost all of whom, in those days, lived in. Instead of a 'hall of residence', they built a huge and massive square tower, six storeys high, with a flat roof and an open parapet—for all the world like a Norman keep.

At that time the iron heel of Cromwell was firmly upon the neck of Scotland. That distressful country was enjoying almost the only spell of strong, just, and decent government that she had known since the happy days before the War of Independence; but no one knew what would happen when Cromwell died. Aberdeen had suffered terribly in the civil wars, so perhaps the King's College professors were anxious for the safety of their young charges. Or perhaps they built the only thing that occurred to them to build.

XI
Bastard Feudalism and a New Kind of Castle

IN describing the Edwardian castles I mentioned the practice of employing paid professional soldiers instead of the short-term feudal levies, and how the standing garrisons which had thus to be maintained affected the plan and inside arrangements of the castles. In the fourteenth century it became common practice for the great barons to keep bands of professional soldiers permanently in their pay, even during peace-time. These soldiers wore their master's livery, and were bound to support him in all his enterprises: not only if he was called upon to lead his forces to join the King in a national war, but also in his private quarrels. Whenever he chose to make an armed raid on a neighbour's land, or to bully the judge and jury in a lawsuit in which he was interested, these liveried retainers were always there to hand for his purpose. The lord was of course bound to maintain them—to support and protect them against all legal or other consequences of their misdoings.

Thus arose the practice known as 'livery and maintenance', by which the great lords kept up private armies of liveried retainers, and maintained them in all their deeds of violence. Usually a powerful baron would do this by entering into indentures with his vassals. By such an indenture the vassal bound himself, in return for his lord's protection, to serve him in all his quarrels with the force of retainers whom the vassal kept in his pay. For example, in 1449 the Earl of Salisbury entered into such an indenture with one

'BASTARD FEUDALISM' AND A NEW KIND OF CASTLE

of his vassals, Walter Strickland. In return for a yearly salary and a share of the spoils, Walter bound himself to keep a force ready to go anywhere at home or abroad, at his lord's command. The force which Walter kept in his pay comprised 290 men, mounted and unmounted. By making a series of such indentures with his vassals, a great lord could soon have a sizeable army at his disposal. The ready money to pay these mercenaries was easily obtained because the lords were now accepting rents paid in cash from their tenants, instead of military service or payments in kind.

In Scotland, such indentures were known as bonds of manrent, because the lord rented the services of armed men to support him in his quarrels.

So everywhere in the fourteenth century, alike in Britain and the Continent, there arose a new kind of feudalism, which once again, as in the bad old days of King Stephen, placed armed power in the hands of the great barons and enabled them to plunge the country into anarchy and to challenge the power of the Crown. In Scotland, during the weak reigns of the kings who followed Robert Bruce, and in England under the misgovernment of Edward II and during the minority of his son, the new practices of livery and maintenance kept the country in a constant uproar. When Edward III embarked on his great war of conquest in France, it was largely by means of such liveried retainers that his battles were fought.

After the death of Henry V the English lost their power in France, and had to cope with large numbers of unemployed ex-service men, used to violence and caring little for the law. An inexhaustible supply of recruits was thus available to the turbulent barons for keeping up their private armies; so there was a new outbreak of feudal anarchy, which in the end led to the Wars of the Roses. In that struggle the feudal barons—like the Kilkenny cats in the fable—finally destroyed each other; and public order in the end was restored by the strong kings of the Tudor dynasty. In the Paston letters there is a vivid picture of the disorder caused in the English countryside by this new kind of feudalism, even before the Wars of the Roses had broken out.

The system is known as *Bastard Feudalism*, to distinguish it from the real thing. We have now to look at the effect which this new kind of feudalism had upon the castles. It meant first that

'BASTARD FEUDALISM' AND A NEW KIND OF CASTLE

every important castle had to provide quarters for standing garrisons, and that these uncomfortable neighbours must be housed separately from the lord's own family and his personal servants; and it meant that the lord had to take special measures for securing the entrance to his castle, in case of treachery among his paid retainers—'men without ruth or conscience, distrusted even by their employers, whose trade was war and whose gain was plunder'.[1] It will be useful to look at some examples of how these two needs were met in practice.

Of all English castles which I have seen, I like most Bodiam in Sussex; chiefly because of the almost unearthly beauty of the ruined castle and its surroundings (Plate 9). In 1917 it was bought by Lord Curzon, who repaired the ruins, put the artificial lake in which they stand and the beautiful grounds into order, and when he died, bequeathed the whole thing to the nation. He also wrote a book about the castle, which was published after his death. In it Lord Curzon describes Bodiam as 'the most romantic and the most fairy of English castles':

'The spectacle of its grey and battlemented walls, with their formidable towers, and fanciful machicolations, all but intact externally (since the interior damage cannot be seen until we have passed the great gateway and entered the court), as they rise proudly from the bosom of a lily-decked moat, so large as to be almost a lake—is unequalled for picturesque beauty among the castles of our own or almost any other country. . . . No trace of the modern world appears to invade the ancient and solitary beauty of the scene; and it could hardly surprise anyone, were a train of richly clad knights, falcons on their wrists, and their ladies mounted on gaily caparisoned palfreys, suddenly to emerge from the barbican gate, for the enjoyment of the chase, or even were the flash of spearheads and the clatter of iron-shod hooves to indicate the exit of a party with more serious intent.'[2]

Bodiam Castle was built by one of the distinguished knights of his time, Sir Edward Dallyngridge, a veteran of the third Edward's French wars. We know its date exactly; for the licence to build it was granted to Sir Edward by Richard II on 20 October 1385. The

[1] G. T. Clark, *Mediaeval Military Architecture in England*, Vol. I, p. 46.
[2] *Bodiam Castle*, pp. xi-xii.

'BASTARD FEUDALISM' AND A NEW KIND OF CASTLE

licence empowers him 'to strengthen with a wall of stone and lime, and crenellate and construct and make into a castle his manor-house of Bodyham, near the sea, in the county of Sussex, for defence of the adjacent country and resistance to our enemies'.

So this castle of Bodiam was built for purposes of national defence, during an invasion scare. Under the weak government of Richard II, England had lost command of the sea. France, Scotland and Castile were all at war with her, and the French and Castilian fleets were victoriously sweeping the Channel. A French landing was thought to be imminent. All round the coast of England strong measures were taken for defence. In London, alarm was great. The shire levies of the Midlands were massed around the capital: those of Kent and Sussex watched the Channel shore; and a fleet of sorts, hastily scraped together, rode uneasily at anchor at Sandwich and Dover.

Under such conditions Sir Edward Dallyngridge would have been bound to maintain a standing garrison in his new castle at Bodiam. Over the rearward gate of the castle, carved in stone, are the arms of the chief under whom he had served in the French wars. This was the famous soldier, Sir Robert Knollys. That warrior had earned himself a fearful reputation in France, where the roofless gables of the countless houses he had destroyed were given the grim nickname 'Knollys's mitres'. Of him, a French writer says that 'he was well worth a hundred thousand crowns, and kept with him many soldiers at his wages; they plundered and robbed so well, that many were glad to follow him'.[1] We may be sure that Sir Edward Dallyngridge did not put the Knollys arms on his castle gate merely as a graceful compliment to his old commander. I have no doubt they were put there in acknowledgement of his feudal superior, and that Sir Edward, in the fashion of the new feudalism, had indentured himself to Sir Robert Knollys. Like Walter Strickland, he would have brought his own contingent of followers to swell the ranks of his chief's private army: a force, perhaps, of 'free companions'—like the 'White Company' in Conan Doyle's story of those times. When not serving abroad, these veterans would be available to provide the standing garrison in his new stronghold. And if we carefully examine Bodiam Castle we shall find that it was ingeniously designed just for this purpose.

[1] Froissart's *Chroniques*, ed. S. Luce, Vol. V, p. 95.

'BASTARD FEUDALISM' AND A NEW KIND OF CASTLE

At first glance the plan of the castle looks extremely simple. Its thick and lofty curtain walls form a rectangle, having stout drum towers at the four angles, a square tower on each flank, and imposing machicolated gatehouses in front and rear. As seen from the outside, all these walls and towers are practically entire, and no castle in Britain gives a greater external impression of feudal power and warlike strength. Inside only the shell remains of the inhabited rooms which once enclosed the courtyard. Studying the ruins closely one finds that there are two sets of apartments, placed back-to-back with each other, and having no communication between them. One is for the owner and his household. It extends round the south, east, and eastern half of the north sides of the quadrangle, and contains, in regular order, the lord's kitchen, hall, great chamber, solar and chapel. On the west side of the quadrangle are separate quarters for the garrison, with their own kitchen and hall. The isolation of the two groups is carefully preserved on all floors of the castle. The lord has the two gatehouses, the cellarage, and the castle well all under his own control.

The gatehouse at Bodiam does not contain the lord's private rooms in the same way as the keep-gatehouse of the Edwardian castles, but it is connected with and controlled from the lord's rooms. And it has a rear portcullis and rear gates closing against the courtyard, so that the entrance could be secured in the event of trouble among the garrison. The postern gate is wholly under the lord's control.

Before leaving Bodiam, it is worth while to notice the way in which the castle was approached across its broad moat or lake. At present one reaches it by an earthen causeway coming directly up to the great gatehouse from the north, but this is modern. On the west side of the moat, near its north end, is a large stone pier or abutment. Down to this pier came the old road leading from Bodiam Church; and from the pier a wooden bridge, resting on trestles, ran across to an octagonal islet cased with stone, which lies in the middle of the moat opposite the gatehouse. Thus the approach to the castle was from the left, and an enemy advancing along the bridge would expose his right side, unprotected by his shield, to the defenders. The foundations of this bridge were found in the mud when Lord Curzon excavated the moat.

From the octagon another bridge led over to a barbican tower, also in the moat, immediately in front of the gatehouse. The barbican was strongly fortified, and had a portcullis. Behind this an earthen causeway extends far enough out for the gatehouse drawbridge to be dropped upon it.

Another wooden bridge, this time on stone foundations, led across from the postern tower to the opposite bank. Probably the foundations of this bridge were heavier because it had to support heavy goods coming in to the castle from the harbour—a basin cut in the bank of the River Rother on the other side which keeps in the water of the moat.

One final word about Bodiam. In the gatehouse, for the first time, we find portholes for firearms. Some were for culverins, an ancient form of small-bore cannon, others for hand-guns. A castle might try to defend itself with the new weapon in this way, but only small guns could be mounted inside or on top of its towers, and when large battering cannon came into use the death-knell was sounded for the feudal castle. Curiously enough one of these bombards, as the early battering guns were called, was found in the moat at Bodiam. A replica of it is inside the castle.

Moving from southern England to the Firth of Forth, on a mighty rock thrust out northward into the sea we find the vast ruin of Tantallon Castle, the great stronghold of the Douglases. It was first mentioned in 1374, and there is no doubt that the existing building, apart from later alterations, belongs to about that time. The Earls of Douglas were then the most powerful men in Scotland. With their private army they bullied the feeble kings of the Stewart dynasty, and held the whole country in a state of terror. Of the sixth Earl it is told that he never rode abroad except at the head of a force of a thousand and sometimes even two thousand men. These were the days of which men truly said that 'nane durst strive wi' a Douglas, nor yet wi' a Douglas's man'.

Earl Douglas could not have gathered such a private army from his feudal tenantry, or there would have been no one left to till the ground; obviously they were his paid livery-men. One old writer declares they were recruited from thieves and murderers and what were then known as 'broken men'. His castle of Tantallon is perfectly designed to house a garrison of such gentry.

Tantallon is equally celebrated for the part it plays in Scott's

'BASTARD FEUDALISM' AND A NEW KIND OF CASTLE

Marmion, where there is such an accurate description of the castle that it may well be quoted here:[1]

> 'But scant three miles the band had rode
>   When o'er a height they passed,
> And, sudden, close before them showed
>   His towers, Tantallon vast;
> Broad, massive, high, and stretching far,
> And held impregnable in war.
> On a projecting rock they rose,
> And round three sides the ocean flows,
> The fourth did battled walls enclose,
>   And double mound and fosse.
> By narrow drawbridge, outworks strong,
> Through studded gates, an entrance long,
>   To the main court they cross.
> It was a wide and stately square:
> Around were lodgings, fit and fair,
>   And towers of various form,
> Which on the court projected far,
> And broke its lines quadrangular.
> Here was square keep, there turret high,
> Or pinnacle that sought the sky,
> Whence oft the Warder could descry
>   The gathering ocean-storm.'

Approaching Tantallon, one is astonished by the enormous curtain wall which with its rock-cut ditch in front straddles the promontory from side to side. At either end is a round tower, and in the centre the Mid-Tower, a square gatehouse which, as in the Edwardian castles, served also as a good dwelling for the lord or castellan.

Inside, on the left is a stately group of domestic buildings. It has been altered, but there must originally have been two halls, one above the other. The lower hall is on the ground floor, with its door in the centre and fireplace opposite, in the middle of the back wall. There was no division into screens, body of the hall, and dais for the lord's table. Obviously this was a barrack hall, like the one at Llanstephan—a mess-room set aside for the Douglas's paid retainers, known as jackmen from the jacks or leather jerkins,

[1] *Marmion*, canto. V, xxxiii.

'BASTARD FEUDALISM' AND A NEW KIND OF CASTLE

strengthened with iron plates, which they wore when riding abroad on their lord's tyrannical errands.

On the other hand, the hall above is approached at the screens end by a broad open stair of state, and is entered by a richly carved doorway. This must have been the lord's festal hall. Here in times of peace the Douglas and his household dined in state; but when war approached his post must surely have been in the Mid-Tower, with the entrance passage in his own safe keeping.

Doune Castle, near Stirling, is another fine structure of the same period of Tantallon. It was built about the close of the fourteenth century by Robert Stewart, Duke of Albany, the regent of Scotland during the long captivity of James I. The castle is practically entire, and has been re-roofed in modern times. In some ways it is the most interesting and instructive castle in Scotland.

The plans (Fig. 28) show three remarkable features of this castle. See also the view, Plate 10.

In the first place, the whole weight and mass of the building is concentrated on the entrance front—the only part where, in this peninsular site between two rivers, a regular assault was to be feared. This implies a much more aggressive kind of defence than in the thirteenth-century castles where living quarters and the donjon or keep were usually in the most inaccessible corner of the courtyard.

Another point worth noticing is that the home of the lord of the castle was combined with the gatehouse as in the English keep-gatehouses of about the same period. And although the inner portal of the gatehouse passage has been altered by modern repairs, there is evidence that it possessed a gate closing against the castle courtyard; which was also in the manner of a keep-gatehouse.

The builders of the older castles seem to have felt that the attack was probably stronger than the defence, and planned against the time when the attackers would force an entry into the courtyard; but the commander of Doune Castle sat in his action-station facing the enemy, on top of the entrance passage, the whole defensive tackle of which was controlled from his own quarters. If the enemy won entrance on another side of the castle, he was prepared to hold it against attack from front and rear.

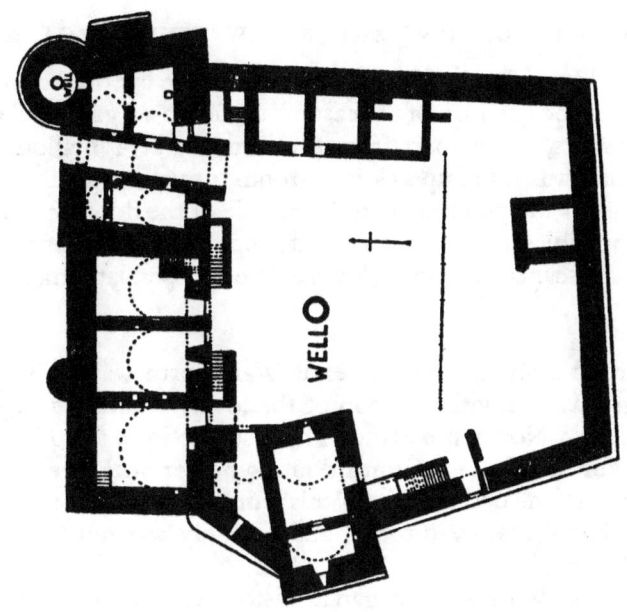
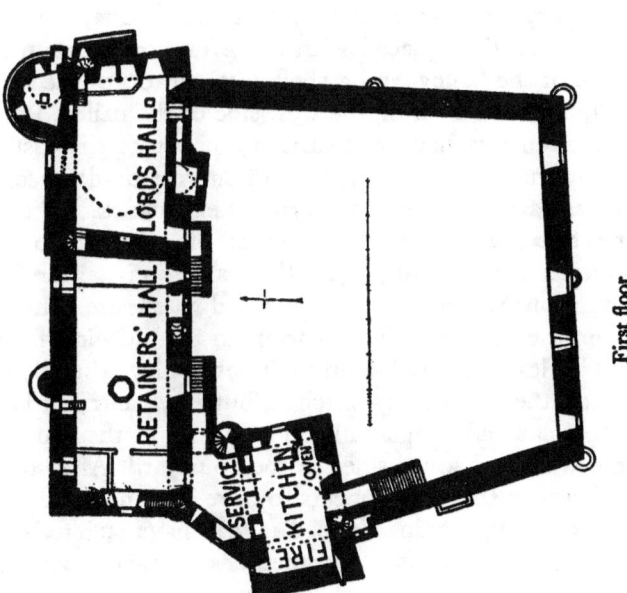

FIG. 28. Doune Castle: plans.

'BASTARD FEUDALISM' AND A NEW KIND OF CASTLE

The third special point about Doune is that the liveried retainers who formed the garrison of the castle had their own great hall and living quarters, quite apart from the lord. As at Tantallon, the garrison hall was fitted up as a mess-room, not a banqueting hall. Its fire was on an open hearth in the middle of the floor, so that as many as possible of the soldiers could keep themselves warm at it. The smoke escaped through a louvre, like an open lantern, in the roof.

The proud castle of the Percies at Warkworth was built high upon a green bluff within a loop of the lovely wooded valley of the Coquet, in Northumberland. Three scenes in *Henry IV* take place at Warkworth Castle; but I doubt whether Shakespeare had ever seen it, for he describes it as 'this worm-eaten hold of ragged stone'. It is not that even today, and certainly was not so in the reign of Henry IV.

The castle of Warkworth began its history as a mount and bailey on a large scale. The bailey is tacked on to one side of the *motte*, and it has the shovel-shaped form often found in such cases. In the twelfth century the timber defences on these Norman earthworks were at least partly replaced with stone: a stone curtain round some parts of the bailey, and a shell-keep on top of the *motte*. A stone hall, too, was built on the west side of the bailey. Probably these improvements had been carried out before the castle was captured by the Scots in 1173, for in that year its defences were described as partly of stone and partly of earthwork.

In the thirteenth century the lords of Warkworth rebuilt or completed the walling in of the bailey on a grand scale, with flanking towers and a fine embattled gatehouse. They came down from their inconvenient quarters in the old Norman shell-keep, and built for themselves in their new bailey, a stately group of rooms on the usual plan—kitchen, buttery, pantry and larder, great hall, solar and chapel, all following on in the usual order round the west and south sides of the courtyard. After this, the old shell-keep on the *motte* appears to have been neglected. Probably it even fell into ruins. Indeed it may have suffered from a slipping of the foundations, as sometimes happened when stone buildings were set on an artificial mount. A small piece of the old shell wall, containing a postern, which still survives on the *motte*,

'BASTARD FEUDALISM' AND A NEW KIND OF CASTLE

embodied in the later building there, is badly warped and cracked by subsidence.

In 1332 the barony of Warkworth passed from the Claverings into the hands of the Percies. That warlike race of barons was charged with the defence of the eastern march against the Scots. During the incessant wars Warkworth Castle became of great importance as a frontier post, and had to admit within its walls an almost constant garrison of jackmen and hobelars. Like other owners of castles at that time, the Percies felt the need for providing new, safe and self-contained quarters for their retinue.

The de Clares in their mount-and-bailey castle of Tonbridge had faced the same problem. There also, in the thirteenth century, the lords had come down from their shell-keep high upon the *motte*, and rehoused themselves in a more spacious way within the bailey. Both the de Clares and the Percies turned over their new domestic buildings to their retainers; but whereas at Tonbridge the de Clares built for themselves a fine keep-gatehouse, at Warkworth the Percies climbed back up the old *motte* again. There they built themselves a tower-house on an extraordinary plan, to which there is no close parallel in England. A coat of arms on the new building shows that it was done before about the year 1390. It must therefore be assigned to Henry Percy, third lord of Warkworth and first Earl of Northumberland, the father of Hotspur.

The donjon or tower-house at Warkworth is a building of the most fascinating interest. Its shape is remarkable, like a large square from which the four corners have been clipped, leaving blunt or canted angles. At the centre of each side of the square is another, smaller projecting building, and if the outer angles of these four projections are cut off in the same way, the result is a plan of the Warkworth donjon. The design was well fitted for its place within the circular area on top of a *motte*.

The donjon has three storeys, which provided elaborate and luxurious quarters for a noble and his personal household. On the ground floor are capacious vaulted cellars and a kitchen, on the first floor are the kitchen, hall, chapel and great chamber. The hall, kitchen and chapel all rise through two storeys, while over the great chamber is a parlour. All these rooms are most cleverly arranged round a central open space which, rising through the whole height of the building, supplies borrowed light to the inner rooms and passages. It also collects the roof drainage, and all the rainwater was thus gathered into a large stone tank in the basement. From this tank the sewers of the tower-house were flushed. Such a short description can give little idea of the ingenious arrangement and clever contrivance shown in the donjon of this Warkworth tower-house.

As the lord's residence, it was kept in repair so long as the castle was occupied. In fact, some rooms in it are still roofed and furnished for the Duke of Northumberland when he visits Warkworth. But the older dwelling house in the courtyard fell into decay when there was no longer need for a standing garrison in the castle. By 1608, only five years after the Union of the Crowns, it was described as 'in great decaye, the hall cleane downe, and nothing left but walles: the kitchen, great chamber, chapell and some other rooms very ruinous'.[1]

The castle is entered now by the great gateway in the south front, from which one goes the whole length of the bailey, with the domestic buildings to the left, and the mighty tower-house in front, high on top of the *motte*. Before reaching the *motte* progress is barred by the foundations of a great cross-shaped church, straddling the courtyard from side to side. It was never completed, and when its remains were dug out, quantities of carved stones fresh from the mason's bench were found lying about. Clearly they had never been built into position.

It will be remembered that castle and church often started off on their lives together, the parish church originally as the private chapel of the castle; but the parish church was apt to fall behind. Each succeeding Norman lord would do his best to enlarge and beautify his castle, yet he was not always so willing to spend money on his parish church. In the twelfth and thirteenth centuries, the piety of the barons more usually expressed itself in the foundation of great monasteries which then were rising in all parts of the land; or in contributing to the building of noble cathedrals which lay within or adjacent to their estates.

But when the Percies took in hand the remodelling of Warkworth Castle, the fashion in church-giving had changed once again. The new fashion was to found a collegiate church; one which was served by a college or body of priests, dwelling to-

[1] *Northumberland County History*, Vol. V, pp. 68–70.

gether in its precincts under a provost or master. Such priests were bound to sing masses and to pray for the soul of the founder of their college, and of any others whom he might name in his deed of gift. A collegiate church of this kind was usually placed quite close to the patron's castle. By their very nearness, the college priests were more intimately bound to pray for the souls of the founder and his family than were the monks in their distant monastery or the chantry priests in the cathedral.

It was in this way that the Dukes of York founded the fine collegiate church which still exists beside their castle of Fotheringhay —though the castle itself, except for Norman earthworks, has all but vanished. So also, close beside the great brick tower which the Lord Treasurer Cromwell added to his castle of Tattershall, and which still survives although almost all else has disappeared, we find a splendid collegiate church which is one of the glories of East Anglia. In Scotland, hard by the castle of the Sinclairs at Roslin is the renowned collegiate church, one of the marvels of Scottish Gothic.

In a few cases the collegiate church was placed actually within the castle courtyard. This may be seen at Hastings Castle, and it is what Sir John Fastolf planned to have in his castle at Caister, though his executors failed to carry out his will. But the best-known example of this is St. George's Chapel at Windsor, a collegiate church of which the canons who serve it live together in a cloister attached to their chapel.

Thus the Percies planned a collegiate church within their castle court at Warkworth. As at Caister, their intention was never fulfilled. If the church had been completed, it may be that Warkworth Castle with its mount and bailey plan, its broad array of walls and towers enclosing the cruciform college church, and its mighty donjon crowning the *motte*, would have become a kind of Windsor of the north.

The castle of Raglan in Monmouthshire is another example of an early Norman layout which was adapted to serve the needs of Bastard Feudalism. Under its earliest lords, who bore the curious name of Bloet, Raglan Castle consisted of a *motte* carved out of a natural hump of marl, enclosed by the usual ditch, and having a bailey of rounded outline extending to the north-west of it. As

'BASTARD FEUDALISM' AND A NEW KIND OF CASTLE

so often happened, the timber defences and domestic buildings of the bailey were in due course replaced in stone. A gate-tower was built at the south-west corner, close to the *motte* ditch; and on the opposite or north-eastern side of the bailey was laid out a hall, with the usual attendant buildings. Parts of these early stone structures still survive in the Fountain Court of the present castle, which occupies the area of the Norman bailey.

I think it likely that by about 1400 the *motte* had been wholly abandoned. But, just as at Warkworth, it was reoccupied and converted into the strong-point of his castle by Sir William ap Thomas, who married the heiress of Raglan in about 1406, and died in 1445. He was a typical example of the 'over-mighty subject' whose power rested on his private force of liveried retainers. For example, in 1441 he assisted his own candidate for the priorship of Goldcliff by seizing the priory with a force of eighty jackmen, casting the rival prior into irons, and forcing him in this brutal way to abandon his claims. In national politics, Sir William led the opposition in Monmouthshire to the House of Lancaster. His son supported the Yorkist cause in the Wars of the Roses, and Edward IV duly showed his gratitude by creating him first Lord Herbert. With other great barons of his time, Lord Herbert engaged extensively in commerce, and acquired vast wealth. He completed his father's reconstruction of Raglan Castle on a magnificent scale.

The ancient *motte* was reoccupied and crowned, just as at Warkworth, with a strong stone tower-house forming a self-contained dwelling for the lord; only here the tower-house entirely encloses the stump of the *motte*, so that its base is a mass of solid marl. The tower-house forms a hexagon, containing in four storeys, each of a single room, the lord's kitchen (with a well), hall, solar, and bed chamber. Perhaps there was even a fifth storey. The old Norman ditch was enlarged and provided with a vertical stone retaining wall on its outer side. It was also filled with water. Access across this great and wide moat was given by a double drawbridge, a broad one for parties and goods, and a narrow one for a single person. Such a drawbridge is more usual on the Continent than in Britain.

A second or retainers' court was constructed to the north-east of the old Norman bailey. The early stone hall then divided the two courts, and the drawbridge leading across to the lord's tower

13. Muness Castle: view from South-East
(See p. 150)

14. Noltland Castle: view from South-East
(See pp. 149, 150)

'BASTARD FEUDALISM' AND A NEW KIND OF CASTLE

was reached only through the solar at the upper end of the hall. So the retainers had no direct access to the lord's tower.

These fifteenth-century buildings at Raglan were constructed in the most magnificent manner, expressing the wealth and dignity of the first Lord Herbert. The walls were built of hewn stone, and the towers, which are multangular, are crowned with superb machicolations. The whole thing must be accounted a great parade of pride in stone. All the towers are equipped for defence both by archery and firearms.

Raglan Castle underwent a second and still more splendid transformation in the reign of Elizabeth, but the new buildings and alterations made at that time do not come within the scope of this book. During the Civil War, it became famous for its heroic defence in the cause of Charles I by its owner, the Marquis of Worcester. Upon its surrender, the castle was 'slighted'—dismantled so thoroughly as to make it useless for military purposes. Two whole sides of the Great Tower were brought down by undermining. A gallery was driven underneath them and the masonry above supported by timber props. The gallery was then packed with combustibles: these were fired, the props burned through, and the two sides of the tower came crashing down!

The increasing turbulence and anarchy of the baronage in the fifteenth century, which culminated in the Wars of the Roses, led to the erection of a number of new castles and the strengthening of others, in parts of England where castle building had become an almost forgotten art. There is no space here to describe the beautiful brick castle built by Sir Roger Fiennes at Herstmonceux in Sussex—now the residence of the Astronomer Royal; Sir John Fastolf's brick castle at Caister in Norfolk, which is really a copy of a *Wasserburg*, or moated castle of the Rhineland; the mighty brick tower (Plate 11) which Lord Treasurer Cromwell added to his Lincolnshire castle of Tattershall; and Lord Hastings's moated castle of brick at Kirby Muxloe in Leicestershire. The use of brick instead of stone was now becoming fashionable in England; and a castle built of this material was not necessarily weaker than one built of stone. When Hull was fortified in the reign of Richard II, its walls, with their thirteen towers, were all made of brick.

But there is one more of the newer English castles which should be described briefly. Scott's account in *Ivanhoe* of the Gentle and Joyous Passage of Arms of Ashby-de-la-Zouch, and of the banquet given by Prince John in the castle there, when the Prince and his Norman favourites were so insolent to his Saxon guests, is well known. Of Ashby-de-la-Zouch Castle, Scott wrote thus:

'This was not the same building of which the stately ruins now interest the traveller, and which was erected at a later period by the Lord Hastings, High Chamberlain of England, one of the first victims of the tyranny of Richard the Third, and yet better known as one of Shakespeare's characters than by his historical fame.'[1]

But in spite of this, quite a lot of the present castle dates back to the early Plantagenet period. In particular, as I have said already (p. 51), the noble hall may be accepted as the place in which Prince John is supposed to have given the famous tournament feast. It was on 17 April 1474 that William, first Lord Hastings, received a licence from Edward IV to new-build and fortify his manor-house of Ashby-de-la-Zouch in Leicestershire. What he found there was an arrangement of hall, great chamber, kitchen, offices, and a large chapel, all linked together by a fortified enclosing wall. He proceeded to add to this an imposing tower-house, placed on the opposite side of the courtyard from the older domestic buildings. This tower formed by itself an isolated, self-contained residence for the lord of the castle and his personal household. Evidently the older domestic buildings were turned over for occupation by his armed liverymen. For like all the nobles of this turbulent period, Lord Hastings kept his private army. In the very year of his licence to fortify Ashby, we find him entering into a bond with two lords, nine knights, and forty-eight esquires, who pledged themselves to aid him against all persons within the kingdom, and to raise as many men as they could, to be armed at his expense!

This great tower of Lord Hastings is not only a strong and ample house for a powerful nobleman, but also one of the most beautiful towers in England. Unhappily half of it was cast down by Parliament in 1646, just as at Raglan Castle. As at Raglan, the walls were crowned with a magnificent, brow-beating machicolated parapet, and at the angles were tall octagonal corbelled turrets, elaborately ornamented, and carried up through two full

[1] *Ivanhoe*, Chap. XIV.

'BASTARD FEUDALISM' AND A NEW KIND OF CASTLE

storeys. The only communication between this tower and the older buildings is by an underground passage, but I believe this may have been made during the Civil War.

At Ashby-de-la-Zouch we are reminded again of how much English life stems from the feudal manor. The name of the borough shows that it grew up under the patronage of the Norman lords of the castle. Immediately north of the castle ruins stands the parish church, once the private chapel of the lord. As we have it today, the church, dedicated to St. Helen, is largely the product of a lavish remodelling by the first Lord Hastings, the builder of the tower-house. In it is the sumptuous white marble monument of a later lord of Ashby, Francis, second Earl of Huntingdon. The whole church breathes the atmosphere of a place of worship which has flourished under the patronage of a noble family. There is a curiosity at the west end of the church, a finger pillory, for the punishment of offenders against ecclesiastical discipline. Hard by church and castle is yet another ancient institution that owes its origin to the lords of Ashby: the former building of the Grammar School, founded by the third Earl of Huntingdon in 1567. Hence the town with the right of a market granted in 1219; its church providing for the religious welfare of the inhabitants and also for most of what we should now call its social services; and the grammar school affording to its brighter children the opportunity of higher education, may all be regarded as the offspring of the feudal castle. Thus a medieval castle was often much more than a baron's stronghold; it could be the seed of local institutions and of local government.

On 14 June 1483, while attending a meeting of the Privy Council in the Tower, Lord Hastings was suddenly arrested by order of the Duke of Gloucester (afterwards Richard III). Without even the pretence of a trial, he was hurried downstairs and out into the courtyard, and his head was there and then hacked off upon a log. The scene is included in Shakespeare's *Richard III*:

> 'O bloody Richard! miserable England!
> I prophesy the fearfull'st time to thee
> That ever wretched age hath look'd upon.
> Come, lead me to the block: bear him my head:
> They smile at me who shortly shall be dead.'[1]

[1] *Richard III*, Act III, Sc. v.

'BASTARD FEUDALISM' AND A NEW KIND OF CASTLE

As a result of his sudden death, work was stopped at the remarkable moated castle of brick which he was then constructing for himself at Kirby Muxloe, not far from Ashby. By a lucky chance the building accounts of Kirby Muxloe have been preserved, with a fullness of detail not excelled in any other instance. They are in Latin, but a translation is available. It is altogether fascinating. We can watch the progress of the building from day to day, from Monday, 23 October 1480, when the first forty cartloads of wood were delivered at the brick kiln, until Monday, 6 December 1484, when all work ceased. Since the news of Lord Hastings' death reached Kirby Muxloe three days afterwards, building had been done only on a very reduced scale. But during all those four years every penny of expenditure, whether in wages of men or purchase of materials, is faithfully recorded. If the good clerk's Latin failed him, he would help himself out with French or English. So we have one delicious entry: *una mucfforke empta pro le ffermyng*. Here we have, in six words, all three main ingredients which have mixed to make the English language.

XII
The Twilight of Castles in England

It was the Tudor despots who put an end to Bastard Feudalism—and, with it, to the English castle. The barons had rent themselves to pieces in the Wars of the Roses, their ranks had been thinned and their power reduced by death in battle or upon the scaffold, by forfeiture of estates and by the ruinous cost of maintaining private armies. The Commons, sick of the disturbance caused by these feudal broils, were happy to entrust great powers to the hands of the King, if he would act as a kind of Chief Constable, suppressing baronial hooliganism and maintaining public order. A different way of life had begun. Many of the barons, like Lord Herbert at Raglan, were seeking wealth by entering into commerce, which requires peace and order if it is to flourish. Others were finding a new pleasure in nursing their estates, in developing agriculture and stock-raising on their farms, in adorning their residences with plantations and well-kept grounds. Others again were interested in buying for themselves beautiful things, fine furniture and tapestries, gold and silver vessels, glass for their tables, beautiful books in print or in manuscript, pictures and works of art.

At the same time, heavy guns had come into use in warfare. These could batter down the strongest castle from outside, but they could not readily be mounted inside a castle, or on top of its towers and walls, as an aid to defence. Moreover, the Tudor monarchs were careful to retain in their own hands a monopoly of casting great guns, and of making gunpowder. This gave the King an enormous advantage in keeping his barons in order. As a schoolboy neatly put it in answering an examination question: 'Also in those days the king had all the gunpowder in the country under him, and that is why the monarchy rose to such a height at this period'!

By Act of Parliament Henry VII prohibited the practices of livery and maintenance. Attempts to do this had been made long before Tudor times: the first statute against maintenance was enacted so far back as 1327, the first against livery in 1377; but the first Tudor king was strong enough to see that these Acts were obeyed. 'As to riot and retainers,' wrote Francis Bacon, in his *Life of Henry VII*, 'there passed scarce any Parliament in this time without a law against them: the King ever having an eye to might and multitude.'[1] How rigorously Henry VII enforced the statutes against livery is strikingly revealed by a story that Bacon tells about the King's visit to the Earl of Oxford at Castle Hedingham:

'At the King's going away, the Earl's servants stood (in a seemly manner) in their livery coats, with cognisances, ranged on both sides, and made the King a lane. The King called the Earl to him, and said "My Lord, I have heard much of your hospitality, but I see it is greater than the speech. These handsome gentlemen and yeomen, which I see on both sides of me, are sure your menial servants." The Earl smiled, and said: "It may please your Grace, that were not for mine ease. They are most of them my retainers, that are come to do me service at such a time as this, and chiefly to your Grace." The King started a little, and said "By my faith (my lord) I thank you for your good cheer, but I may not endure to have my laws broken in my sight. My attorney must speak with you." And it is part of the report that the Earl compounded for no less than fifteen thousand marks.'[2]

The point is that if all these men had been the Earl's paid household staff, as Henry pretended to think they were, there would not have been the least objection to his having as many as he could afford to pay, and to their wearing their employer's monogram or coat of arms. But in his reply, the Earl confessed that this was not the case. He could not afford to keep up so large an establishment of servants. The men who formed the King's guard of honour

[1] Ed. 1622, p. 216.   [2] *Ibid.*, p. 211.

were not Lord Oxford's personal servants, but his retainers in the old bad sense. Each of them had accepted an obligation to be his man, to turn out in his livery and to follow him when required, under the system of indenture which I have described. It was this political and military relationship between a lord and his indentured retainers that had now been made illegal; for this the Earl of Oxford had to suffer.

Under the strong Tudor monarchy, then, no more castles in the old sense—the private strongholds of feudal lords having military power at their command—were allowed to be erected. Probably the last castle, in the real meaning of the word, to be built in England was Thornbury in Gloucestershire. It was begun in 1511 by Edward Stafford, third Duke of Buckingham, of whom it was said that he had designs upon the throne. He was accused of accumulating arms and munitions, and of recruiting men for his private army in Wales, which lies just across the Severn from the castle which he had begun to build at Thornbury. In 1521 Henry VIII thought the rumours sufficiently disquieting to order the Duke's arrest and trial. Buckingham lost his head, and his castle remains unfinished to this day.

Thornbury Castle is one of the most remarkable buildings in England. It was perhaps the last great baronial house to be built in the old castellated style, and retaining something of the serious purpose of medieval fortification. The imposing entrance front, with its central gatehouse and angle towers, all crowned with heavy machicolated parapets, and loopholed for both archery and firearms, preserves much of the stern reality of a fourteenth-century castle like Bodiam. And, as at Bodiam, we find inside that the lord's private dwelling was jealously separated from the rest of the castle, and that the gatehouse with its defences was strictly under his personal control.

In front of the castle is a spacious forecourt, enclosed by long ranges of barrack and stable accommodation, large enough to house a whole regiment of armed retainers; far more than the mere garrisoning of the castle—supposing a garrison to be still necessary at this time—could have needed.

The gatehouse of this forecourt and of the main castle were secured by a portcullis, and the forecourt, like the main castle,

THE TWILIGHT OF CASTLES IN ENGLAND

was equipped for defence with bows and guns. We can easily imagine that King Henry felt the time had passed when country gentlemen should fancy that it was necessary or desirable for them to include portcullises, bowslits, gunloops, and machicolations in their mansion houses. The only kind of fortification he wished to see built in his realm were those which he was putting up himself —the remarkable coastal castles, built to house heavy guns, which he was building along the Channel. Examples of these may still be seen at Deal and Walmer, and elsewhere. They are very curious structures, built in the plan of a quatrefoil, with two or more tiers of casemates for housing cannon. Unlike the tall old castles, they are squat and low, with walls of immense thickness. In fact they are not really castles at all: they were not the private strongholds of a feudal baron, but national fortifications like modern coast defences.

At Thornbury, the west or entrance front of the castle still has much of the stern reality of a medieval fortress. With its multangular towers and the frowning machicolated parapets, it reminds one quite a lot of Raglan. But at the south side, where stood the residential buildings of the lord, all semblance of defensive architecture has vanished. Large and beautiful oriel windows, as fine as any in England, open on the ground floor, and the whole appearance of the house on this side is that of a noble mansion. Doubtless the Duke of Buckingham found it easier to discard security on this side, because here the castle is covered by a massive embattled outer wall enclosing the privy garden, beyond which lie the parish church and churchyard.

The last English licence to crenellate was issued in 1533. It was granted by Henry VIII to Sir William Fitzwilliam, and empowered him, quite in the old language, 'to embattle, fortify, crenellate and machicolate' the walls and towers of his manor-house at Cowdray, near Midhurst in Sussex. But that this language was only a piece of fossil legal phraseology can be seen from the ruins which still exist at Cowdray. The gatehouse and frontal towers have only the external appearance of such. They do not form defensive units in the old fashion, and indeed on the upper floors the gatehouse is wide open to the range extending north from it. So the castellated appearance of Cowdray turns out, in spite of the licence, to be nothing but a sham.

THE TWILIGHT OF CASTLES IN ENGLAND

At Sutton Place, in Surrey, built between 1520 and 1530, the transformation of the castle into the country house has gone a stage further. The gatehouse is now destroyed, but we know its plan, and it was a pure pretence as at Cowdray. At Cowdray there were imposing angle towers, but at Sutton these became no more than gabled frontal projections of the two side wings. It is far on the way to the common type of Elizabethan country house with its central porch and lateral projecting, gabled wings. Such a house resembles in plan the letter E, and is often fancifully thought to portray, in graceful compliment, the initial letter of the Queen's name.

So the strong forbidding castle of the Middle Ages was superseded by the gracious Elizabethan country house. Sometimes a new owner abandoned the stone fortress of his predecessors and rehoused himself in stately fashion in a new brick mansion nearby. At other times, if he still belonged to the old stock and was loath to desert his ancestral seat, he sought to make it more comfortable by altering or adding to it in the new Tudor domestic style. That is what the later Herberts did at Raglan. Such works may be seen in Leicester's buildings at Kenilworth Castle: and, in a most beautiful example, at Carew Castle in Pembrokeshire.

But a glorious end was still reserved for the English castles. In the Civil War their stout old walls, furbished up and often protected by external earthwork bastions for the heavy artillery now in use, proved themselves capable of offering a prolonged resistance to the siege tactics of the time. Many an English castle held in the Royalist cause, like Ashby and Raglan, went down fighting and suffered the inevitable end of 'slighting' at the hands of the victorious Parliament. At Scarborough, Kenilworth, Pontefract— to name only a few instances—we can still see how Roundhead gunpowder concluded a long and honourable history.

Nowhere in England was the fury of the Parliament, in dealing with Royalist castles, more savagely displayed than at Corfe Castle in Dorsetshire. It stands in the Isle of Purbeck, about midway between Wareham and Swanage. The Isle is really a peninsula traversed from west to east by a range of chalk hills a dozen miles long. Midway in this range it is cleft by a great gap, known to the Saxons as Corfe-gate, the road or pass of Corfe. In the centre of this gap rises an isolated hill, and upon this the castle is placed. The situation is thus a most striking one (Plate 12).

The ruins of the castle cover more than three acres. There are three baileys, a lower, middle and upper. In Norman times the upper bailey formed a large *motte*, and on it William the Conqueror built the usual wooden tower. Henry I replaced this by a noble stone keep. Before his time the *motte* had already been walled about with stone, and a stone hall had been built in the middle or western bailey. Part of this hall still remains, a very fine example of herring-bone work.

Under the Plantagenets, and chiefly by Henry III and Edward I, the whole area of the castle was enclosed within a great array of stone walls and towers, including two fine gatehouses, one in the Outer and another in the Middle Ward. In the Upper Ward, on what had been the old Norman *motte*, Henry III built himself a beautiful palace. Even in its shattered ruins, it shows us that the third Henry had more aesthetic taste than most English monarchs. The only other who could rival him in this was Richard II.

Since Corfe was a royal castle, much information about the building work which went on there, from reign to reign, is preserved in the national accounts. Even more fascinating is the amount of knowledge we have about the part which the castle played as the administrative centre of Purbeck. Thus we find that the whole of the Isle of Purbeck formed a royal domain, dependent on Corfe Castle. Every tithing, or group of ten householders, was bound in time of war to provide one able-bodied man to serve for ten days in the garrison of the castle, at the King's wages. Many of the farms were further bound to deliver to the Constable, for the use of the garrison, so many bushels of wheat or cartloads of hay each year. Others were obliged to give him rents in poultry, salt, cumin (an oil-seed), wax, pepper, horseshoes, and other forms of payment in kind. One holding was let on condition that the tenant found a carpenter when required 'to work about the great tower of the castle'. This was the manor of Moulton, near Swanage. In the Conqueror's time it had belonged to Durand, the King's carpenter, who probably was responsible for the erection and upkeep of the original wooden tower on the *motte*. So the feudal obligation which he owed in respect of his land had descended to his successors.

THE TWILIGHT OF CASTLES IN ENGLAND

On his side the Constable enjoyed great privileges. In virtue of his office, he was Lord Lieutenant and Admiral of Purbeck, with power to array the militia. He had, or claimed to have, the right to cut timber and quarry stone throughout the Island for repairs to the castle, and also to gather firewood from unenclosed woods. All flotsam and jetsam—wreckage cast up by the sea—had to be delivered to him. He was entitled to a share of all beer brewed upon the Island, and those tenants who possessed suitable carts were bound to provide carriage from Wareham for the wine that he required. From any wine ships arriving on the coast, he was empowered to exact prisage, which was a right to the compulsory purchase of one tun of wine for every twenty tuns on board. A tun was a measure of liquor equal to 252 gallons. The Constable also had the right to claim all the royal fish—grampuses, porpoises, and sturgeons—caught upon the coast. Furthermore he could claim, on the King's behalf, all nesting falcons in the Island. Those who brought in such royal fish or birds were entitled to a suitable reward. Every fisherman had to pay to the Constable a fee for the licence for his boat.

He also exercised a firm control, through his warreners and rangers, over all game upon the Island. These gamekeepers were entitled, after giving one day's notice, to be supplied with free board and drink, for themselves and their dogs, by every tenant on the Island for one day each week. They had the power to arrest anybody found offending against the game-laws.

How strict was the supervision exerted by the Constable over the inhabitants of the Island is shown by the fact that no tenant could give his daughter in marriage without the Constable's consent.

Feudal justice was administered by the Constable, or by his steward on his behalf, in his barony courts, held in front of the castle gate. There is an old drawing of Corfe, made in 1586, showing the market square in front of the castle gate, with stocks and the pillory. Behind the castle, on a conspicuous knoll overlooking the Wareham road, rises the grim outline of the gibbet.

The town of Corfe formed a royal burgh, dependent on the castle. Its tenants, called barons, had the right to choose their own mayor, coroner, bailiffs and common council, but otherwise they were strictly overlooked by the Constable of the castle. In time

THE TWILIGHT OF CASTLES IN ENGLAND

of war they were bound to give forty days' service in each year in its garrison and during this service they received free beer. Every Saturday they had to carry bread and beer from Wareham to Corfe for the Constable's use. They had the right to hold their own courts of piepowder, where disputes and brawls arising upon market days were decided. The name is derived from the French phrase *pieds poudreux*—dusty feet—from the dusty shoes of those who came to market.

During the Civil War Corfe Castle was twice besieged by the forces of Parliament. On the first occasion, in 1643, it was heroically defended by the owner's wife, Lady Bankes. A portrait shows her as a formidable lady, holding in her hand the keys of the castle, which appears behind her in the distance. The siege was a curious mixture of old and new methods. The assailants tried first to capture the place by the old device of a sow—a wooden penthouse wheeled up against the walls; but the penthouse, being mounted on wheels, did not cover the legs of those inside. The garrison from their flanking towers were able to pepper their shins so thoroughly with musket shot that nine of the eleven poor fellows inside were put out of action, and one was slain outright. Then the besiegers sought to batter their way in with heavy guns. Some of them they mounted on the church tower, using the lead of the church to make bullets, and its organ pipes for cartridge cases. Another battery was planted on the west side of the castle, and its earthworks may be seen there to this day. Next they brought up a detachment of marines armed with scaling ladders, handgrenades and petards[1] for blowing in the gates, and with these aids they attempted to carry the castle by storm. All the marines were made drunk as an encouragement, except the Commander, Sir Walter Earle. He remained sober, so a Royalist chronicler asserts, 'for fear he should be valiant against his will'. But when the scaling ladders were planted, Lady Bankes and her heroic handful were waiting on top of the castle walls with stones and hot embers, and the attackers were repulsed with a loss of a hundred men. Just then, news arrived that a Royalist force was marching to relieve the castle. So, on 4 August 1643, Sir Walter Earle ingloriously called off the siege.

[1] A petard was a kind of portable land mine, fixed to a gate or door, and exploded so as to blow it up.

THE TWILIGHT OF CASTLES IN ENGLAND

In the second siege, which took place in 1646, Lady Bankes was in London, and the castle was defended by Colonel Anketil. In the end it was taken by treachery. Everything inside was plundered by the victorious Roundheads. The list of goods taken shows how sumptuously a great house was furnished in the seventeenth century—in contrast to the simple furniture of earlier days. We read of splendid pictured tapestries, of gilt leather or damask hangings, of satin cushions, Turkey and Persian carpets, and others made of quilted silk, of a rich ebony cabinet, numerous beds with their luxurious furnishings, trunks full of fine clothes, household linen and damask, of tables and chairs, pots and pans, of books 'all new and good' to the value of £1,300. One large trunk is described as being 'inlaid all over with mother of pearl'.

On 5 March 1646 Parliament ordered that Corfe Castle should be 'demolished'. The usual word was to 'slight', which implied sufficient destruction of the defences of the place as to make it untenable. The word demolish, used about Corfe, implies that something much more drastic was intended. We may gather from this how greatly the stubborn resistance of the castle had enraged the Roundheads.

Certainly their orders were thoroughly obeyed. Gunpowder was used on an extravagant scale. In this way two-thirds of the keep was blown away, with the astonishing result that the central part of its east wall stands unsupported, to a height of fully 60 feet —a marvel of Norman masonry, as has been truly said. The fragments lie today as they fell in 1646 in a chaos of wild confusion. The beautiful buildings of Henry III were utterly shattered, and stand now only in lovely, piteous fragments. Some of the towers on the curtain walls have been blown out, others have been overturned by mines of the older description, like that which was used on the East Tower of Raglan Castle. Two towers on the west front, undermined in this way, are now tilted forward at a fantastic angle. Another of these mines has split the inner gatehouse into two, so that one tower has settled down to a depth of fully 10 feet, but otherwise remains unbroken and almost vertical. Whole sections of the curtain walls have been lifted forwards, or even bodily overturned. But the destruction wrought at Corfe must be seen to be believed. It remains the most vivid and dreadful picture in England of the devastation caused by the Civil War.

THE TWILIGHT OF CASTLES IN ENGLAND

'The cause in which thy towers did fall
Had brought a blessing on them all
   Did fortune follow worth,
Then when you raised, mid sap and siege,
The banners of your rightful liege
   At your she-captain's call,
Who, miracle of womankind
Lent mettle to the meanest hind
   That manned her castle wall.'[1]

The last English castle to be described here is in some respects the most interesting of all. It has been truly said that 'its walls are stained with the blood of every race which has mingled to make the English people'; for the story of Pevensey Castle illustrates every stage in the coastal defence of England against invaders coming across the Channel, from Roman times to the Second World War.

In the later days of the Roman occupation of Britain the Angles and Saxons, who so soon were to conquer the country, were already making themselves a nuisance by their piratical raids upon the eastern and southern coasts. To meet this danger, the Romans built a series of forts at points along those coasts where the raiders were apt to land. The garrisons of these forts were placed under the command of a general called the Count of the Saxon Shore.

One of these Saxon Shore forts is at Pevensey, on the Sussex coast between Eastbourne and Hastings. Since Roman times the sea has receded, and there is now almost a mile's breadth of green meadow and grey shingle between the fortress and the shore. But when it was built a harbour lay immediately underneath its eastern walls. Before the fort was made, this harbour had for long been used in connection with the export of coastwise traffic of the Sussex iron ore. This is proved by the discovery, on the site of the fort, of pottery and coins belonging to a period much before the organization of the Saxon Shore. Here also, in the early days, the Imperial Navy in Britain had a calling station. The Roman name for Pevensey was *Anderida* or *Anderita*.

Considerable parts of its walls have slipped and fallen, yet a great deal of the Roman fort remains. It forms an egg-shaped

---

[1] W. Stewart Rose, quoted in *The Story of Corfe Castle*, by George Bankes, p. 222.

THE TWILIGHT OF CASTLES IN ENGLAND

enclosure, surrounded by a great wall about 12 feet thick and 27 feet high. This wall is strengthened by a series of solid bastions, having straight sides and rounded fronts. Two of them flank the main gate at the west end of the fort. The area within covers nearly 10 acres.

The walls were built of concrete, made with flints, sandstone fragments and beach pebbles, and faced with smallish blocks of sandstone. In a way which is common in late Roman buildings this facework is varied by horizontal courses of green sandstone, dark ironstone, or red brick. This banded appearance may be seen also in other forts on the Saxon Shore. The mortar used in the facework of the walling was mixed with pounded brick, giving it a lovely pink colour.

A careful look at the walls will show that they were built in sections, by different gangs of soldiers or workpeople, as in the seaward curtain of Dunstanburgh Castle.

When the foundations of some of the fallen bastions were being excavated, it was noticed that they had been built on a kind of raft of wooden beams or sleepers. Of course the wood had long since decayed, but the channels in which these sleepers had rested were still preserved in the foundation layer of flints and chalk. In one of these channels was found a coin of Constantine the Great, the first Roman Emperor who became a Christian. This coin was struck about the year 330. Clearly it must have been lost in the foundation of the bastion before the wooden sleepers were laid. Therefore it seems likely that the fort at Pevensey was not begun before about 330. In 343 the raids upon the coast had become so serious that the Emperor Constans, a son of Constantine, had to visit Britain; so great was the danger that he crossed the Channel from Boulogne in mid-winter. To commemorate this expedition a bronze medal was struck. It seems quite likely that as a result of this visit of Constans the fort of Anderida was built. Most of the coins found here belong to the House of Constantine.

The Roman garrison of Pevensey was a detachment of the Abulci. These are believed to have been heavy infantry from Gaul; but once stationed at Anderida they would no doubt have been recruited locally.

It is most impressive to see this great array of battered, weather-beaten and weather-eaten walls and towers at Pevensey. There they stand, stern and defiant, after sixteen centuries—built by Imperial Rome to keep the English out of Britain.

In the *Anglo-Saxon Chronicle* we have a grim notice of the end of Anderida. This did not come until A.D. 491—eighty-one years after the Emperor Honorius had told the Romanized Britons that they must henceforth provide for their own defence. Here are the words of the *Chronicle*:

'Aelle and Cisse beset Andredes-cester, and slew all who dwelt in it, nor was there one Briton left.'

As a rule it was not the custom of the Angles and Saxons to settle upon Roman sites, or within stone walls. They preferred the open country. So at Anderida they left the old Roman fort unoccupied, and built themselves a village on either side of it. On the east somebody called Peofn settled down with his followers, and so the place got the name of Pevensey, Peofn's island. Later, on the opposite side of the deserted fort another village grew up, and this became known as Westham, the western hamlet. So today the ruins of Roman Anderida stand between two old English villages, Pevensey and Westham, each with its ancient church.

At Pevensey the parish church is dedicated to St. Nicholas, the patron of sailors; another reminder that the hamlet was formerly a port. Indeed, the stretch of the little River Ashburn from Pevensey to the sea is still known as the Haven, though now it finds its outlet through the shingle in an iron pipe. It is hard today to realize that Pevensey was once a corporation and a member of the Cinque Ports. Its diminutive Town Hall yet stands, and the Corporation seal and mace are preserved in the church. At one time indeed Pevensey made its own coins, and an ancient building in the village is still known as the Mint House. On 28 September 1066, William the Norman landed at Pevensey. The great walls and bastions of the old Roman fort must have been the first things to greet him in England.

When England and Normandy were joined in one realm, as they had been in Roman times, the harbour of Pevensey regained its importance as a means of communication between the two lands. So in the south-east corner of the old Roman fort the Normans built themselves a castle. This consisted of a great stone keep, built on a most extraordinary plan, with five projecting bastions clearly imitated from the Roman work. What purpose

15. Craigievar Castle: view from North-West
(See p. 152)

16. Iron Yett at Barns Castle, Peeblesshire
(See pp. 106, 113)

THE TWILIGHT OF CASTLES IN ENGLAND

these bastions served we do not know, for little is left of the Norman keep except its foundations. One bastion contained a deep well, which has its part in one of Kipling's stories in *Puck of Pook's Hill*.

This Norman keep stood within an enclosure consisting of a palisaded bank and ditch. At the same time the old Roman walls and towers were repaired so as to make them into an outer bailey for the castle. We may still see how one of the Roman bastions has been patched with herring-bone work, which is usual in Norman buildings of the eleventh century (Plate 1).

In the reign of King John, Normandy was taken from England by the French. With a hostile power now on the opposite side of the Channel, a strengthening of the coastal defences became necessary; so early in the thirteenth century the Norman ditch of the inner bailey was deepened and widened and turned into a moat, and the palisaded bank replaced by a strong and well-built curtain wall, with round towers and a gatehouse, all beautifully faced with fine masonry (see Fig. 13). The thirteenth-century architects could have held their faces up to their Roman predecessors. In 1264, during the Barons' War, this new castle stood a vain siege at the hands of Simon de Montfort the younger. By that time large portions of the Roman walls had already fallen, so that the old fort of the Saxon Shore no longer counted as part of the defences of the castle.

In the fifteenth century the conquests of Henry V in France once more united both sides of the Channel under a single rule, and the military importance of Pevensey was therefore much diminished. Moreover, by this time the sea was receding, and the harbour was becoming derelict. So the castle was neglected, and by the time of Elizabeth it was in utter ruin. But once again the Armada scare in 1587–8 led to a tightening up of the coastal defences; and again Pevensey had its part to play. Looking out to sea, at a place where the Roman wall had fallen and thus made a great breach in the defences, a gun platform was thrown up. It is still to be seen; and there also lies a cannon bearing the monogram of Queen Elizabeth I—still on the spot to which it was dragged to confront the Invincible Armada, more than three and a half centuries ago.

Today, standing on this Elizabethan gun platform and looking out through the breach in the Roman wall, one sees the modern coastline fringed with a row of Martello towers. These were blockhouses erected as part of the coastal defence arrangements when England was expecting an invasion by Napoleon in the opening years of the last century. They are said to have been so called from Cape Mortella in Corsica, where such a tower made a stout resistance to bombardment by a British fleet in 1794.

In 1940 the coasts of Britain were once more prepared against imminent invasion. Sixteen centuries earlier the fort of Anderida had been erected to keep the Teutons out of Britain; and now once more its walls were brought into commission for the very same purpose. Machine-gun nests of steel and concrete, faced with old stone, so as to look like ancient work, were built on top of some of the Roman and medieval towers. Some of these modern works have been left in position, for surely they are part of the history of the castle.

XIII
The Indian Summer of the Scottish Castle

THE Tudor period ended the era of the English castle, but in Scotland the castle had still a full century or more of vigorous life before it. No such strong monarchy emerged in the northern realm at the close of the Middle Ages. On the contrary, the Stewart dynasty was wretchedly weak, and moreover it suffered from a tragic succession of minorities. Between the accession of James I in 1406, and the Union of the Crowns under James VI and I in 1603, only one Scottish monarch died peacefully in his bed—and he, it is said, of a broken heart. Under these circumstances the feuds of the barons and lairds continued as fiercely as ever, and the kingdom was kept in an uproar. Not seldom, baronial factions fought for the possession of the King, who was liable to be kidnapped and carted about from castle to castle.

The course taken by the Reformation north of the Border also made for instability in Scotland. In England the overthrow of the ancient faith was effected from above. It was carried out by the will of Henry VIII, and upon the whole it was accepted by the people without any serious disorder. But in Scotland the old Church was destroyed by a revolution carried out in the teeth of the government by a handful of zealous reformers in league with a gang of nobles who longed for the Church's lands.

For this reason, the Scottish Reformation was bitterly resisted by large masses of people. So when the Reformers dethroned Queen Mary and set up her infant son, James VI, in her place, the outcome was a savage Civil War which for years kept the whole country in a turmoil. Under cover of religion, or of loyalty to the Queen or to her son, the nobles and their followers fought out their private feuds with one another. During this war deeds of cruelty seldom paralleled in British history were perpetrated by both sides.

It was therefore still necessary for every laird's house to be fortified and equipped for defence by the arquebuses or hand-guns which were now in general use. These late Scottish houses of fence, as they were called, are extremely interesting; and of course there is nothing at all like them in England. They show great cleverness in planning, and the way they were equipped for defence by firearms is most ingenious.

One of the commonest ways of doing this was to provide the central building—whether tower-house or hall-house, with two flanking towers, set at diagonally opposite corners. Thus each tower with its gunloops flanked the sides of the main building, while the main building in its turn covered the towers. It will be seen from the plan (Fig. 27) that it was impossible to approach such a castle from any quarter of the compass without coming under fire.

This is called the Z-plan, an admirable Scottish device by which two towers did the work of four in protecting all four sides of the central house.

Being so logical and economic, the Z-plan became a great favourite in Scotland, particularly in the district round Aberdeen. About seventy examples are known to survive. The flanking towers might be either round or square; sometimes one tower was round and the other square.

These Z castles have about them a certain appearance of sturdy and repelling strength which I find fascinating. They have the look of a boxer, with one arm on guard and the other withdrawn for the punch.

The flanking towers also provided the castle with a great deal of private accommodation, at a time when this was more and more needed. Since the towers were set diagonally they merely touched the main structure, and this way both the main building and the towers interfere as little as possible with each others' lighting.

THE INDIAN SUMMER OF THE SCOTTISH CASTLE

One of the best-preserved Z-castles in Scotland is Claypotts, on the outskirts of Dundee. It bears the dates 1569 and 1588, probably those of commencement and completion. Later, it was a home of John Graham of Claverhouse, Viscount Dundee, the Royalist leader who fell in the moment of victory at Killiecrankie in 1689. To his enemies he was known as Bloody Clavers; to his admirers as Bonnie Dundee. Claypotts is quite a small house, but strongly built, with a vaulted and therefore a fireproof basement. It is well provided all round with gunloops for musketry defence. Here the two flanking towers are cylindrical; but above they are corbelled or bracketed out with square overhanging garrets with the usual Scotch crow-stepped gables. The main house is likewise gabled in this way, and the effect of all this top-hamper is strikingly picturesque, unimaginable anywhere but in Scotland.

By far the most formidable castle on the Z-plan is on the remote island of Westray, in the Orkneys. Its name is Noltland, pronounced Nowtland. Approaching the little haven of Pierowall, where one lands on Westray, it is astonishing to see this large and powerful castle towering up on the hill behind the village.

The builder of Noltland Castle was Gilbert Balfour of Westray, one of the worst thugs in Scotland during the troubled times of Queen Mary. He was one of those involved in the murder of Cardinal Beaton in 1546, and of the Queen's wretched husband, Henry, Lord Darnley, in 1567. At last things became so dangerous for him that he retired to his island estate in Westray, where he had already commenced to build Noltland Castle as a hideout. Even in Westray, however, he could find no safety, so he fled overseas and took service in the Swedish army. But even here he could not restrain his inborn itch for plotting. He joined in a conspiracy against the King of Sweden, and paid for his treason with his life.

From the appearance of Noltland Castle there is no doubt that it was built by a man with fear in his heart. It is of great size, and the two flanking towers are square. Even in its ruined state I have counted no less than seventy-one gunloops in what remains of the building. Most of these are large enough for the guns called falcons, small cannon of $2\frac{1}{2}$ inch bore, throwing a ball of $1\frac{1}{2}$ lb. weight. Many of these gunloops still retain inside, the slot or chase for a wooden baton on which the piece rested. From the outside

THE INDIAN SUMMER OF THE SCOTTISH CASTLE

the grim walls of Noltland Castle, pierced by tiers of these yawning gunloops, look like the hulk of an old man-of-war. Certainly no other British castle displays such formidable equipment for defence by firearms.

The most northerly castle in the British Isles is built upon the Z-plan. This is Muness Castle in Unst, the northernmost island of the Shetlands (Plate 13). Its builder, Laurence Bruce, might well have exclaimed in the words of Longfellow:

> 'So far I live to the northward
> No man lives north of me.'

So far towards the realm of the Midnight Sun, indeed, lies this lovely ruin, that a complete set of plans and drawings of it was once made in the month of June, during the midnight hours.

At Muness Castle the two flanking towers are round (Fig. 29). Over the door is the following delightful inscription:

> 'List ye to know yis building quha began?
> Laurence the Bruce, he was that worthy man
> Quha ernestly his airis and ofspring prayis
> To help and not to hurt this vark aluayis.
> The zeir of God 1598.'

Remote though it is, this castle has not escaped the shock of war. In 1627 it was burnt by a Dutch vessel from Dunkirk. It is interesting to note that in the hearting or core of the walls, bits of brick can be found. To this out-of-the-world castle such a material could have found its way only as ship's ballast.

After the Union of the Crowns in 1603 happier times seemed to be in store for Scotland, though it was to prove but a false dawn.

In the first place, paradoxical though it may seem, the King was able to rule Scotland with a much firmer hand from London than from Edinburgh. In London he was beyond the control of the rival baronial factions, of the violent Edinburgh mob, and of the fanatical Presbyterian ministers who stirred them up into riot and sedition. 'This I must say for Scotland,' said James to his English Parliament: 'here I sit and govern it with my pen. I write and it is done, and by a Clerk of the Council I govern Scotland now, which others could not do by the sword.' From the opposite standpoint

THE INDIAN SUMMER OF THE SCOTTISH CASTLE

we have the lament of honest Mrs. Howden in *The Heart of Midlothian*:[1]

'I dinna ken muckle about the law; but I ken, when we had a king, and a chancellor, and parliament men, o' our ain, we could aye peeble them wi' stanes when they werena gude bairns. But naebody's nails can reach the length o' Lunnon!'

Also the Union of the Crowns, and the fact that both kingdoms, though in different ways, had now followed the path of Reformation in matters ecclesiastical, put an end to the cruel wars which had for so long drained away the wealth and lifeblood of the weaker nation.

Many of the Scottish barons and lairds were in funds as they had never been before. To a large extent the lands and wealth of the ancient Church had fallen into their hands. Like the English barons after the Wars of the Roses, their interests were now turning away from strife and bloodshed. Some of them were entering commerce; others used their new-found wealth to develop their estates, to lay out fine gardens and spacious ground, to acquire learning and to buy books. For example, it is said that the Earl of Dunfermline, Lord Chancellor of Scotland, was 'a great humanist in prose and poesy, Greek and Latin; well versed in the mathematics, and had great skill in architecture and heraldry'.[2] Nor was he the only one of his class. Indeed, many of the smaller Scottish lairds or country gentlemen by this time were men of taste and scholarship, able to give a lead in the Renaissance activities.

So during this tranquil period between the Union of the Crowns and the outbreak of the Civil War in 1638, Scotland was covered with a host of castellated mansions in the Scottish Baronial style. These buildings were still equipped for firearm defence, yet they are really castles only in name. The old open turrets at the angles, used for flanking defence, were now roofed in with the candle-extinguisher or cone-shaped helmets so characteristic of these later Scottish castles. The open parapet on the wall-heads, from which the defenders could hurl down missiles, disappeared. The high-pitched roof now rested directly on the walls as for a modern house. Instead of the old embrasures we have dormer windows to

[1] Chap. IV.
[2] G. Seton, *Memoirs of Alexander Seton, Earl of Dunfermline*, p. 19.

light the garrets; and often they were made with much decoration. For the first time we begin to see the incoming of classical models, and these dormer windows sometimes have little pediments like those of a Roman temple. The roofs are always high-pitched, and lie between crow-stepped gables, with great chimney stacks having moulded copes.

In old English houses the upper storeys often oversail on timber bracketing. In Scotland, where wood was scarce, this oversailing was managed by means of stone corbelling, and this became a characteristic feature of the latest Scottish castles. Often it was used in quite riotous profusion, and in places where it served no useful purpose. In the same way, the weepers or rain-spouts which carried off the wet from the old open parapets were often stuck on now purely as ornament, where there was no possibility of their draining any water. Sometimes the imitation spouts were carved to represent miniature cannon.

These castellated mansions have very rich interiors. Some have beautiful plaster ceilings, in others the ceilings are painted in tempera work—in colours made with a medium soluble in water, like modern distemper. Scotland is specially rich in these painted ceilings.

Space will not allow more than a mention of the more famous among these Scottish baronial mansions. Lord Dunfermline built two of the finest—Fyvie Castle in Aberdeenshire, and Pinkie House near Edinburgh. Other notable examples are Castle Fraser and Craigievar in Aberdeenshire, Crathes in Kincardineshire, Glamis in Angus, and Earlshall in Fife. Taken altogether, these buildings represent an architectural heritage of which any nation might be proud. With them the history of the British castle as a living reality comes to a close. For this Scottish baronial architecture did not survive the Wars of Religion. For a full generation the building of great houses practically ceased throughout the land. When better times returned the old race of masons, bred in the national style, had died out, and the way was open for Scotland to follow her southern partner in the new architecture of the classical Renaissance.

One of the most picturesque of the latest Scottish tower-houses is shown in Plate 15.

XIV
'Gothick' and Modern Castles

AMONG many people in the eighteenth century the Middle Ages were in almost complete disgrace. They were regarded as a time of monkish gloom and barbarism. Their architecture was stigmatized as Gothic, in memory of the Goths who overthrew the Roman Empire, and were accused of having destroyed the civilization of the ancient world. The literature of the Middle Ages, their sagas and romantic ballads, were dismissed as unworthy of the attention of educated men and women. Ruined castles were often regarded with contempt; one writer thought the noble remains of Corfe Castle an object of 'horror and concern'. By the common folk they were avoided from reason of superstition:

> 'The lonely tower
> Is also shunned; whose mournful chambers hold
> (So night-struck fancy dreams) the yelling ghost.'[1]

These were days when many men thought that the only literatures really worthy of imitation, the only architecture worth copying, were from ancient Greece and Rome. Poets imitated the descriptions of natural scenery which they found in Virgil's *Georgics*; for poetry had become largely the product of the town, and those who wrote about nature saw it through a townsman's eyes. In architecture, the fashion was to build country houses with pillared and pedimented porticos like a Greek or Roman temple. Some of the greatest of English mansions, such as the Duke of Marlborough's palace at Blenheim, were built in this Palladian

---
[1] Thomson's *Seasons: Summer*.

'GOTHICK' AND MODERN CASTLES

style. Around such country houses the grounds were laid out formally, often in avenues, circles or quadrants centred on the house itself—a geometrical layout imposed without reference to the natural features of the landscape. Everywhere the ideas of symmetry and classical correctness reigned supreme.

Yet even at the height of this eighteenth-century classicism the old romanticism of the Middle Ages did not perish utterly. The love of nature for its own sake rather than as a background for man, found expression in James Thomson's *Seasons*. In *The Castle of Indolence* he gave the world a 'Gothick' romance, written in the long-neglected Spenserian stanza which itself came as a breeze from a less conventional world. Somewhat later, Percy in his *Reliques* succeeded in reviving interest in the wild ballads of the Middle Ages. Still greater was the enthusiasm roused by James Macpherson's translations of the third-century Gaelic poet, Ossian. Though most of these were Macpherson's own inventions, their influence on the literary world of the time, both here and on the Continent, was tremendous. The vague and cloudy elder world of car-borne heroes, like Fingal and Cuchullin; heroic, suffering ladies like Bragela 'the lonely sunbeam of Dunskaith, viewless spirits riding the tempest; the weird landscape of storm-beaten mountain and windswept moorland—came into the urban literature of the time like country air into a stuffy drawing-room. The tumultuous reception of Ossian was one of the first signs that men were getting weary of the purely classical culture of the eighteenth century.

So it is not quite surprising that during this period one or two great houses were built in imitation of a medieval castle. Those who built them were trying, quite deliberately, to revive the long-neglected Gothic style of architecture. Since they wrote the word with a 'k', we may use the term Gothick, so spelt, to denote this eighteenth-century revival, or imitation, of the real Gothic of the Middle Ages.

One of the most striking examples of this Gothick architecture of the eighteenth century is Inveraray Castle, the seat of the Duke of Argyll. It was built by an architect called Roger Morris between 1746 and 1765, but the interiors were not completed until 1783, and then by a different hand. The castle consists of a rectangular structure with round towers at each corner, and a great square

'GOTHICK' AND MODERN CASTLES

tower in the middle, rising high over all. Clearly the architect was trying to reproduce a French château of the fourteenth or fifteenth century. The windows and doors have pointed arches. But if the outside is Gothick, the interiors, as completed twenty years later, are in the most fashionable classical style of the period, and as bright and full of graceful elegance as the exterior is gloomy and ponderous.

Scotland can show an even more remarkable Gothick building in Culzean Castle, Ayrshire. This is the seat of the Marquis of Ailsa, but he has handed it over to the National Trust for Scotland. Culzean Castle was built between 1777 and 1782, to the designs of Robert Adam. At Culzean he designed, externally, a Gothick castle which has been described as 'rising up sheer from the sea to the height of a hundred feet, brandishing its castellated towers and bastions like the stronghold of a pirate king'.[1] But as at Inveraray, the interiors were designed, decorated, and finished in Adam's usual classical manner; and no lovelier rooms than some of them can be found among all his work.

No doubt it was the romantic landscape of his native Scotland, the wild country of the Cheviots, that inspired Thomson to turn back to nature for its own sake. No doubt also the picturesque sceneries of Argyllshire and of the Ayrshire coast played their part in suggesting the sham castles of Inveraray and Culzean. But England also has its essays in the Gothick manner.

Lacock Abbey in Wiltshire is an example where the beautiful remains of a thirteenth-century nunnery are embodied in a sixteenth-century mansion which shows splendidly the earliest or Italianate phase of the Renaissance in English architecture. About 1753-5 some of the interiors of this house were decorated in the Gothick manner. It looks thin and wiry, quite unlike real Gothic work; yet it is full of charm, and deeply interesting. Lacock Abbey, with the lovely village nestling at its gates, now belongs to the National Trust for England.

At the other end of England, Craster Tower in Northumberland, a fourteenth-century tower-house with an addition of the eighteenth century has similar Gothick interiors, of great curiosity

[1] J. Fleming, *Scottish Country Homes and Gardens Open to the Public*, p. 90.

'GOTHICK' AND MODERN CASTLES

and beauty. But the best-known example of Gothick building in England was Horace Walpole's mansion on Strawberry Hill near Twickenham. It was the counterpart of his Gothick novel, *The Castle of Otranto*, which really started the Romantic Revival.

The Romantic Revival was the final revolt of educated folk in Western Europe against the classical spirit that had dominated the eighteenth century. In Britain, in literature the way had been prepared by the writing of Thomson, Percy, Macpherson, Walpole and others. But its beginning may be dated to the appearance in 1805 of Scott's *Lay of the Last Minstrel*, which revealed to the men and women of that time the long-neglected wonder and romance of the Middle Ages.

Scott's other romantic poems that followed, and then the majestic sequence of the *Waverley* novels, created an enormous sensation. People went quite mad about the Middle Ages. Indeed, in 1839 the Earl of Eglinton and his friends actually got themselves into armour and engaged in a mock tournament like the 'Gentle and Joyous Passage of Arms of Ashby'. This tournament cost the noble lord more than £30,000. One of the knights who jousted on that occasion was the future Emperor Napoleon III. The Queen of Beauty was Lady Seymour, a granddaughter of Sheridan. The tournament was quite a real affair, the knights splintering their spears against each other just like Bois Guilbert and Ivanhoe. Unfortunately for the gallant knights and fair ladies, it poured with rain the whole day.

With men in this spirit, it was only natural that up and down the country the mouldering ruins of long-abandoned castles should be restored and made habitable, or that other landowners should build themselves new mansions in the castellated style. Once started, the fashion lasted until the Second World War. So in England we have such notable restorations as Herstmonceux Castle in Sussex, now the residence of the Astronomer Royal; Allington Castle, Hever Castle and Leeds Castle, all in Kent; Sudeley Castle in Gloucestershire, or Caldicot Castle in Monmouthshire. Best known of all was Sir Jeffry Wyatville's restoration of Windsor, which has already been described (see pp. 93–4). In Wales there are Cardiff Castle and Castell Coch in Glamorgan. In Scotland some notable restorations were carried out between

'GOTHICK' AND MODERN CASTLES

the two World Wars by Sir Robert Lorimer, the architect of the Scottish National War Memorial in Edinburgh Castle. Perhaps the best of these is Dundarawe Castle on Loch Fyne, Argyllshire.

At the same time other landlords were building themselves modern castles. In England the most astonishing of these is Peckforton Castle in Cheshire. In Wales we have Penrhyn Castle, in Caernarvonshire, built in the Norman style; and in Scotland many lairds' houses were built or remodelled in the Scottish baronial style. The most famous of these is Balmoral, erected for Queen Victoria and the Prince Consort between 1853 and 1856. Almost as notable is Scott's Abbotsford—though here, very curiously, the author of *Waverley* did not build in the Scottish baronial style, but in a curious mixture of his own ideas of Gothic and Tudor.

But the days of all this are now over. The wealth in private hands which restored or built these castles has been destroyed by ruthless taxation. It is safe to prophesy that no more castles will be restored, and no new castles built by private money, in Britain ever again. Indeed, many of the existing ones are being abandoned by their owners, and pulled down for the sake of their materials. Awakening all too late to the grievous loss which our national heritage is thus suffering, the State is endeavouring to save some of the others by giving grants of public money to their owners to enable them to keep them in repair, and so to continue living in them. But there remains the cost of upkeep, and the difficulty of finding household servants. So it is clear that the day of the castle as a residence is over. Of those in ruins, an increasing number are now beautifully maintained by the Ancient Monuments Division of the Ministry of Works. Many others are fast disappearing, so the story is coming to an end.

Explaining castles has been my delight for more than fifty years. I hope I have managed to show in this book something of the fascination to be found in time spent that way.

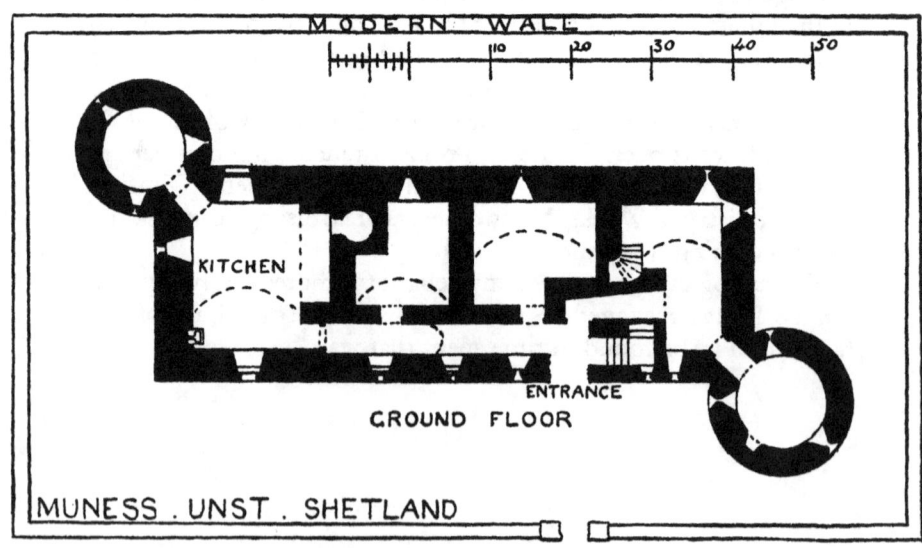

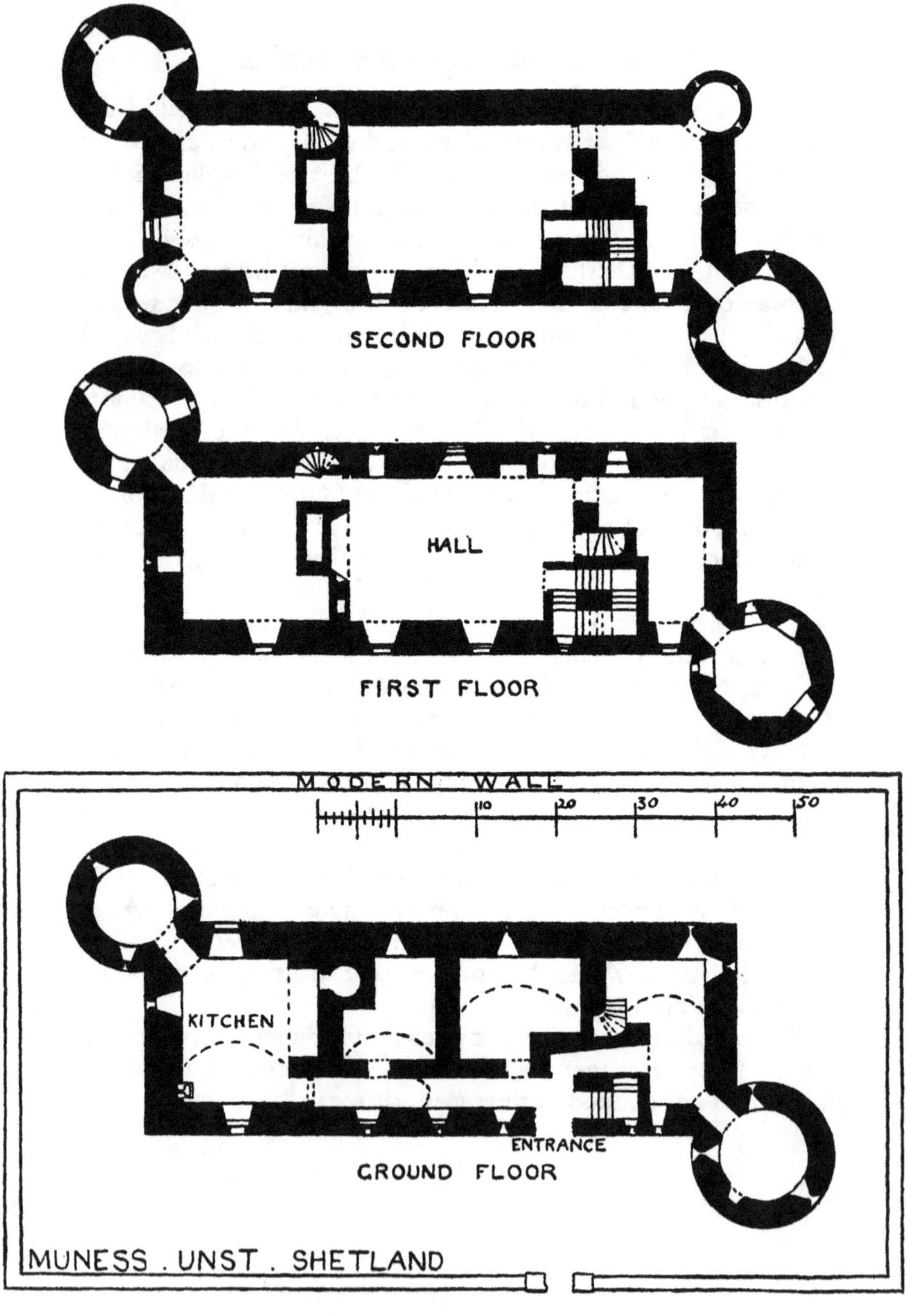

FIG. 29 Muness Castle: plans.

Index

Abbotsford, 157
Aberdeen, 114, 148
Aberystwyth, 62
Aboyne, 96
Abulci, 143
Acre, Joan of, 76
Adam, Robert, 155
Agincourt, 22
Aigues Mortes, 59
Ailnoth, 90
Alaric, 10
Albany, Duke of, 122
Allington, 156
Anderida, 142
Anketil, Colonel, 141
Appleby, 73
Armada, the Invincible, 145
arquebus, 148
artillery, 71, 111, 130, 133, 134, 135, 136, 137, 140, 145, 149
Arundel, 6
Ashby-de-la-Zouch, 51, 130, 137
ashlar, 14
Aydon, 51, 101–2

bailey, 5, 73, 76, 90, 124, 127, 128, 138, 145, 158
Balfour, Gilbert, 149
Balmoral, 157
Bamborough, 14
Bankes, Lady, 140, 141
Bannockburn, 101
barbican, 26, 49, 105, 119
barmkin, 105, 107
Barnwell, 50
Barons' War, 145
'bastard' feudalism, 115–33

bastides, 57, 59, 84
Bayeux Tapestry, 7
Beaton, Cardinal, 149
Beaumaris, 62, 63, 71
Becket, Archbishop, 52
belfry, 21, 22, 23, 24
Belsay, 109, 110
Blenheim, 153
Bodiam, 117–20, 135
Bolton, 54
bombard, 120
bonnet laird, 114
Bordeaux, 68, 96
Bordland, 9
Borthwick, 109, 110
Bothwell, 24, 48
brattice, bretasche, 15, 21
brick, 129, 150
Bruce, Laurence, 150
Builth, 71
Bute, Marquis of, 68
buttery, 51

Caernarvon, 22, 57, 63, 64, 65, 66, 69, 70, 71, 90, 94, 95, 102
Caerphilly, 53, 66, 67, 68, 69, 73
Caerwent, 84
Caister, 127, 129
Caldicot, 156
Camulodunum, 18
Cardiff, 6, 156
Carew, 137
Carisbrooke, 19
Carlisle, 14, 18
Castell Coch, 156
castle guard, 27
Castleton, 9

INDEX

castle work, 84
cat, 21, 24
catapult, 22
Charles I, 59, 92
Charles II, 93
Château Gaillard, 49, 61, 62
Chipchase, 107, 108, 109
Chirk, 71
Christ Church, Oxford, 11
Civil War, 68, 129, 130, 131, 137, 140, 141, 151
Clare, Gilbert de, 66, 69, 71, 76
Claverhouse, 149
Claypotts, 149
Clifford's Tower, 48, 54
coastal castles (Tudor), 71, 136
Cobbie Row's Castle, 14, 55
Colchester, 14, 18, 19
Colle, Nicholas de, 96, 97
collegiate churches, 126, 127
concentric castles, 61, 62, 63, 66, 67, 68, 87
Conisborough, 45, 47, 48, 61
Constans, 143
Constantine the Great, 143
Constantinople, 71
Conway, 22, 57, 63, 69, 70, 71
corbels, 15, 85, 152
Corbridge, 101, 103-4
Corfe, 19, 54, 137-41
Coull, 95, 96
Cowdray, 136
Coxton, 111-14
Craigievar, 152
Craster, 156
Crathes, 152
Crécy, 22
crenellation, 102, 118, 136
Criccieth, 71
Cromwell, Lord Treasurer, 127, 129
Cromwell, Oliver, 87, 111, 114
crossbow, 20, 22
Crusades, 42, 45, 87, 96
culverin, 120
Culzean, 155
curtain walls, 7, 42, 43, 87, 90
Curzon, Lord, 117

dais, 11, 52
Dallyngridge, Sir Edward, 117, 118
Danes, 86
Darnley, Lord, 149
Deal, 136
Denbigh, 69, 70
Dirleton, 42
Dolwyddelan, 71
donjon, 49, 61, 62, 63, 73, 122, 125
Douglas, Earls of, 120
Doune, 122-4
Dover, 15, 18, 27, 29, 118
Duffus, 6, 7, 48, 95
Dundarawe, 157
Dundee, Viscount, 149
Dundonald, 56
Dunfermline, Lord Chancellor, 151, 152
Dunstanburgh, 80-5, 143
Durand, 138
Durham, 8

Earlshall, 152
Edinburgh, 157
Edward I, 24, 50, 54, 55, 56, 57, 66, 70, 76, 77, 87, 90, 91, 94, 95, 96, 138
Edward II, 43, 53, 99, 116
Edward III, 8, 89, 92, 116
Edward IV, 92, 128
Edward VII, 92
Earle, Sir Walter, 140
Eglinton Tournament, 156
Elias, Master, 84
Elizabeth I, 71, 137, 145
Embleton, 80
embrasure, 15, 102, 103

falcons, 149
Fastolf, Sir John, 127, 129
feudalism, 2-3, 77-8, 115-32
Fiennes, Sir Roger, 129
Fitzscrob, Richard, 55
Fitzwilliam, Sir William, 136
Flemington, 9
Flinders, 9
Flint, 57, 58, 59, 62, 71

INDEX

forework, 15, 31
Forth, Firth of, 84, 120
Fotheringhay, 127
Framlingham, 45
Fraser, 152
Fyvie, 152

Garter, Knights of the, 92
Gaunt, John of, 82
Gaveston, Piers, 101
George III, 92, 93
George IV, 93
George V, 92
George VI, 92
Glamis, 152
Glendower, Owen, 59
Glendearg, 103
Goldcliff, 128
Gothic Revival, 93, 153–6
Greenknowe, 107
gunpowder, 133, 134, 141

half-timber work, 89, 102
hall-house, 11, 12, 51, 109
Harlech, 51, 57, 59–62, 71, 73
Hastings, 8, 127
Hastings, Lord, 129–32
Hedingham, 4, 14, 15, 134
Henry II, 29, 48, 87, 90
Henry III, 24, 26, 30, 35, 54, 55, 66, 76, 87, 90, 91
Henry V, 145
Henry VI, 92
Henry VII, 92, 134
Henry VIII, 71, 89, 92, 135, 147
Herbert, Lord, 128, 129, 134
herring-bone masonry, 19, 138
Herstmonceux, 129, 156
Hever, 156
Hexham, 101
hoarding, 15, 16, 21
hobelars, 83, 125
Honorius, 144
Hotspur, 125
Hull, 57, 84, 129
Huntingdon, Earl of, 131
Huntingtower, 85

indenture, 114, 115, 135
Ingliston, 9
Innes, Sir Alexander, 111
Inveraray, 154
Invernochty, 6
Isabella, Queen, 99
Ivanhoe, 26, 48, 51, 93, 130

jackmen, 121, 125, 128
James I, 122, 147
James VI, 147, 150
Jerusalem, 84
Jerusalem, Church of Holy Sepulchre at, 55
joggled construction, 88
John, 25, 29, 30, 45, 52, 90, 130, 145

keep, 13–19, 45, 48, 49, 55, 61, 73, 86, 99, 114, 122
keep-gatehouse, 55, 62, 73–5, 78, 82, 83, 119, 122, 125
Kenilworth, 24, 45, 137
Kent, Earl of, 100
Kidwelly, 68, 79
Kildrummy, 43, 51, 56
King's College, Aberdeen, 114
Kirby Muxloe, 129, 132
Knollys, Sir Robert, 118
Kolbein Hruga, 14
Krak des Chevaliers, 87

Lacock, 155
Lacy, Henry de, 69, 84
Lay of the Last Minstrel, 156
Leeds, 156
Lewes, 6
Lewyn, John, 54
Lincoln, 19
Linlithgow, 25, 26
livery and maintenance, 115, 116, 134
Llanstephan, 79, 80, 82, 85
Llewelyn-ap-Gruffyd, 66
Loches, 44
Lochindorb, 50
Lochwood, 105
London, Temple Church, 55

INDEX

London, Tower of, 4, 14, 16, 18, 19, 54, 86–90
longbow, 20, 22
Longthorpe, 98–100
Lorimer, Sir Robert, 157
Louis IX, 59
louvre, 52
Lucca, 96
Ludlow, 55, 73

Macduff's Castle, 85
machicolation, 85, 109, 114, 117, 119, 129, 130, 135, 136
Madoc-ap-Llewelyn, 62
Mains, 9
maintenance, *see* livery and maintenance
majolica ware, 96
manrent, 166
Martello towers, 146
Mary Queen of Scots, 147, 149
Maurice, 29
merlon, 15, 102
meurtrière, murder hole, 16, 19, 61, 65, 75, 80
mine, 25
Monkchester, 28
Montfort, Simon de (younger), 145
Morris, Roger, 154
motte, 5, 9, 12, 13, 19, 48, 63, 73, 76, 86, 90, 94, 95, 124, 125, 126, 127, 128, 138
Moulton, 138
Muness, 150, 158

Napoleon, Prince Imperial, 92
Newcastle-upon-Tyne, 4, 14, 15, 18, 26, 28–41, 109
Noltland, 149, 150
Norham, 4, 14
Norwich, 14

Orford, 48
Orphir, 55
Orvieto ware, 96
Orwell, 99

Ossian, 154
Oxford, Earl of, 134, 135

palace, *palatium*, 11
Palladian style, 153, 154
pavise, 20, 21
Peckforton, 157
peel, 104
Pembroke, 48
Penrhyn, 157
Percy, Henry, 125
Perpendicular style, 92
petard, 140
Pevensey, 19, 45, 46, 84, 142–6
piepowder, 140
Pinkie, 152
'pit', 3, 18
Plantagenet, Thomas, Earl of Lancaster, 80, 83
Pleshy, 5
Plessis-les-Tours, 31
polychrome jugs, 68, 96
Pons Aelius, 28
Pontefract, 137
Porchester, 18
portcullis, 25, 61, 65, 73, 80, 107, 119, 120, 135, 136
prisage, 139

quarrel, 20

Raglan, 127–9, 130, 137, 141
Raymes, Robert de, 101, 102
re-entrant angle, 106, 107
Reformation, 147
Reynes, Henry of, 54
Rhuddlan, 62, 71
Ricciardi, 96
Richard I, 48, 52, 87
Richard II, 12, 117, 118, 138
Richard III, 131
Richard's Castle, 55
Robert I, 95
Robert Curthose, 28, 29
Rochester, 4, 16, 17, 25, 45
Romantic Revival, 156
Roscrea, 85

INDEX

Roses, Wars of the, 116, 128, 129, 133
Roslin, 127
Rothesay, 25
Ruthin, 71

Sandwich, 118
Saxon Shore, 71, 142
Scarborough, 137
Scottish baronial style, 151
Scott, Sir Walter, 31, 93, 156
screens, 11
shell-keep, 19, 29, 73, 124
Shrewsbury, 6
'slighting', 129, 137, 141
solar, 11, 98, 107
sow, 24, 140
spence, 103
Stafford, Edward, 35
St. Andrews, 25, 85
Stephen, 8
St. George d'Esperance, 70
St. George, James of, 54, 59, 70, 71, 94, 95
Stewart, Robert, Duke of Albany, 122
Strawberry Hill, 156
Strickland, Walter, 116
Sudeley, 156
Sutton, 137
Sutton Hoo, 10
Swin, 14

table dormant, 52
Tamworth, 19, 29
tempera painting, 152
terra mensalis, 9
Tantallon, 120–2
Tattershall, 127, 129
Thomas, Sir William ap, 128

Thomson, James, 154, 155
Thornbury, 135–6
Thorpe, William de, 98
Tibbers, 50, 56
Tickhill, 6, 19
Tonbridge, 6, 19, 29, 71–7, 82, 85, 125
Torquilstone, 26
tower-house, 12, 98–114
Trevoux, 70

Union of the Crowns, 126, 150, 151
Urr, 6

Vikings, 12
villes neuves, 57, 59

Walmer, 136
Walpole, Horace, 156
Wareham, 139
Warkworth, 124–7, 128
Waverley novels, 156
Westham, 144
Westminster Abbey, 54, 55
Westminster Hall, 11, 12
William I, 2, 14, 28, 86, 90, 138, 144
William II, 73, 86
Winchelsea, 57
Winchester, 55
Windsor, 8, 29, 54, 86, 90–3, 127, 156
Worcester, Marquis of, 129
Wyatt, James, 93
Wyatville, Sir Jeffry, 93, 156
Wyre, 14, 55

'yett', 106, 113
Yevele, Henry, 54
York, 48, 54

For Product Safety Concerns and Information please contact our EU representative GPSR@taylorandfrancis.com
Taylor & Francis Verlag GmbH, Kaufingerstraße 24, 80331 München, Germany

www.ingramcontent.com/pod-product-compliance
Lightning Source LLC
Chambersburg PA
CBHW052121300426
44116CB00010B/1760